I0004294

Mastering Artificial Intelligence

Learning Artificial Intelligence

Edition 2

By Joshua Moses

Copyright © 2024, Joshua Moses

All rights reserved. No part of this book may be copied, reproduced, stored, or transmitted in any form or by any means—electronic, mechanical, photocopying, recording, or otherwise—without prior written permission from the publisher, except in the case of brief quotations used in reviews or critical articles.

Table of Contents

Chapter 1: Introduction to Artificial Intelligence

Let's have a good, long chat about this fascinating world of Artificial Intelligence, or AI as most folks call it. Now, don't let the name intimidate you. It might sound like something straight out of a sci-fi movie with robots taking over the world, but the reality, at least for now, is a whole lot more nuanced and, honestly, pretty darn interesting. Think of it less like sentient machines plotting world domination and more like really clever software that can learn and solve problems, kind of like how we humans do, but in its own unique way.

At its heart, AI is all about creating computer systems that can perform tasks that typically require human intelligence. Now, that's a broad statement, isn't it? What exactly does "human intelligence" entail? Well, it's a whole cocktail of things: learning from experience, understanding language, recognizing patterns, making decisions, solving problems, and even things like creativity. AI aims to mimic some, or even all, of these abilities in machines.

Imagine teaching a child to recognize different kinds of animals. You show them a picture of a dog and say "dog." You do this a few times with different breeds, and eventually, the child starts to understand the general concept of "dog-ness" – furry, four legs, often barks. They can then apply this understanding to identify a dog they've never seen before. That, in a very simplified way, is similar to how some AI systems learn. We feed them tons of data, like thousands of pictures of dogs, and they start to pick up on the patterns and characteristics that define a dog.

Now, AI isn't some monolithic entity. It's more like a big umbrella term that covers a whole range of different approaches and technologies. You might hear terms like machine learning, deep learning, neural networks – these are all different tools and techniques within the broader field of AI. Think of it like the different tools in a carpenter's workshop. A hammer, a saw, and a chisel are all tools, but they serve different purposes. Similarly, these different AI techniques are used to tackle different kinds of problems.

Machine learning, for instance, is a big one. It's basically about training computers to learn from data without being explicitly programmed for every single task. Instead of writing a specific set of instructions for every possible scenario, you feed the system data, and it learns to identify patterns and make predictions or decisions based on that data. That animal recognition example we talked about? That's a classic application of machine learning.

Then you have deep learning, which is a more advanced subset of machine learning. It uses artificial neural networks with many layers (hence "deep") to analyze complex data like images, speech, and text. These neural networks are inspired by the way our own brains work, with interconnected nodes that process information. Deep learning has been behind some of the really impressive AI feats you might have heard about, like self-driving cars getting better at navigating roads or voice assistants understanding your sometimes mumbled commands.

It's important to understand that AI isn't magic. It relies heavily on data. The more good quality data you feed an AI system, the better it generally becomes at its task. Think of it like trying to learn a new language. The more you hear, read, and speak the language, the more fluent you become. It's a similar principle with AI.

Now, you might be thinking, "Okay, that sounds kind of technical. Where do I actually see AI in my daily life?" And the answer is, probably more than you realize! Think about the recommendations you get on streaming services for movies or music – that's often AI at work, analyzing your past viewing or listening habits to suggest things you might like. When you use a search engine and it autocompletes your queries or shows you the most relevant results, that's AI in action. Even spam filters in your email are a form of AI, learning to identify and filter out unwanted messages.

AI is also being used in all sorts of industries, from healthcare to finance to manufacturing. In healthcare, it can help doctors analyze medical images to detect diseases earlier. In finance, it can be used to identify fraudulent transactions. In manufacturing, it can optimize production processes and predict equipment failures. The possibilities are really quite vast.

Of course, with any powerful technology, there are also important considerations. Things like bias in the data used to train AI systems can lead to unfair or discriminatory outcomes. Ensuring fairness, transparency, and accountability in AI development and deployment is a really important area of ongoing research and discussion.

So, in a nutshell, AI is about creating intelligent computer systems that can learn, reason, and solve problems. It's a field with a rich history and a rapidly evolving present, and it's already woven its way into many aspects of our lives. While the idea of truly sentient AI might still be the stuff of science fiction for now, the practical applications of AI are very real and are likely to become even more integrated into our world as time goes on. It's a journey of discovery, and we're really just at the beginning of understanding its full potential.

Defining AI and its Goals

Let's dive a little deeper into what we actually mean when we talk about "defining" Artificial Intelligence and what folks in the field are generally trying to achieve with it – its goals, if you will. It's a bit like trying to define "intelligence" itself, which, as you can imagine, can get pretty philosophical and a little bit slippery. But we can certainly paint a clearer picture of what AI is striving to be and what problems it's setting out to solve.

When we try to pin down a definition for AI, we often come back to this idea of creating machines that can perform tasks that, if a human were to do them, we'd say require intelligence. Now, that's still a pretty broad stroke, isn't it? Think about all the things we humans do that we consider intelligent – from playing chess to understanding a joke, from diagnosing a medical condition to writing a poem. AI, in its various forms, tries to tackle different slices of this vast spectrum of human cognitive abilities.

So, instead of one neat, tidy definition, it's perhaps more helpful to think of AI as a field of study and development focused on enabling computers and machines to think, learn, and act intelligently. That "intelligently" part is key, and it's where things get interesting. What does it really mean for a machine to be intelligent?

One way to think about it is in terms of capabilities. Can the machine learn from data, like we discussed before? Can it reason logically to solve problems? Can it understand and process natural language, like when you talk to a voice assistant? Can it perceive its environment and make decisions based on that perception, like a self-driving car navigating traffic? These are all hallmarks of what we consider intelligent behavior, and these are the kinds of capabilities that AI researchers and engineers are trying to build into machines.

Now, let's talk about the goals of AI. What are the driving forces behind all this research and development? Well, at a very fundamental level, a major goal is to understand intelligence itself. By trying to build intelligent systems, we can gain deeper insights into how our own minds work. It's almost like trying to understand how a bird flies by building an airplane. The airplane isn't a bird, but the process of designing and building it can teach us a lot about the principles of aerodynamics that also govern bird flight. Similarly, building AI systems can give us new perspectives on the nature of intelligence, learning, and problem-solving.

But beyond just understanding intelligence, there are a whole host of practical goals driving AI research. One big one is automation – creating systems that can perform tasks more efficiently, accurately, and sometimes even faster than humans. Think about those robotic arms in factories that can assemble products with incredible precision, or algorithms that can process massive amounts of data to identify trends that a human analyst might miss. AI has the potential to automate many repetitive or complex tasks, freeing up human workers to focus on more creative, strategic, or interpersonal roles.

Another key goal is to augment human capabilities. It's not always about replacing humans entirely, but rather about creating tools that can enhance what we can do. Think about those medical diagnosis AI systems again. They don't replace doctors, but they can act as powerful assistants, helping to analyze scans and patient data to provide doctors with more information and potentially improve the accuracy of diagnoses. Similarly, AI-powered language translation tools can help people from different linguistic backgrounds communicate more effectively.

Improving decision-making is another significant goal. AI systems can analyze vast amounts of data and identify patterns that can inform better decisions in various fields. For example, in business, AI can help predict customer behavior or optimize supply chains. In environmental science, it can help analyze climate data to understand and predict environmental changes. By providing data-driven insights, AI can help us make more informed and effective choices.

Then there's the goal of creating more personalized and adaptive systems. Think about how streaming services recommend content tailored to your tastes or how personalized learning platforms can adapt to a student's individual learning pace and style. AI enables the creation of systems that can understand individual needs and preferences and respond in a more relevant and helpful way.

And of course, we can't forget the more ambitious, long-term goals. Some researchers are striving towards what's often called Artificial General Intelligence, or AGI. This refers to AI systems that would possess human-level cognitive abilities across a wide range of tasks – the ability to learn, understand, and apply knowledge just like a person. While we're still quite a ways off from achieving true AGI, it remains a fascinating and driving aspiration for many in the field.

It's also important to recognize that the goals of AI are not static. As the field progresses and we develop new capabilities, our aspirations and the potential applications of AI also evolve. What might have seemed like science fiction a few decades ago is now becoming a reality, and as we continue to push the boundaries of what's possible, the future of AI and its goals will undoubtedly continue to surprise and inspire us.

So, to bring it all together, defining AI is about recognizing its pursuit of intelligent behavior in machines. Its goals are multifaceted, ranging from understanding intelligence itself to automating tasks, augmenting human capabilities, improving decision-making, personalizing experiences, and ultimately, perhaps one day, achieving a more general form of intelligence. It's a dynamic and exciting field, constantly striving to create systems that can learn, reason, and act in ways that we recognize as smart and helpful.

Our Fascination Intelligent Machines

You know, when you really stop and think about it, this whole drive to create intelligent machines, this fascination that has captured the imaginations of scientists, engineers, writers, and just generally curious folks for generations, it's a pretty profound thing. It taps into some really fundamental aspects of what it means to be human, our desire to understand ourselves, our place in the universe, and our innate urge to build and innovate.

Think back way before computers even existed in the way we know them now. The idea of creating artificial beings, things that could think or act on their own, has been around for centuries. You see it in myths and legends, in stories of automatons and magical creations. There's this long-standing human curiosity about whether we could imbue inanimate objects with some form of life or intelligence, almost like playing God in a way, but also driven by a deep desire to understand the very essence of consciousness and thought.

Then, as science and technology progressed, this fascination started to move from the realm of pure fantasy into something that felt potentially achievable. The development of computers, these incredible machines that could process information and follow complex instructions, really sparked the modern era of AI. Suddenly, the idea of creating something that could truly think didn't seem so far-fetched anymore. It was like we had finally found the raw materials to start building our intelligent creations.

Part of the allure, I think, comes from this mirror that AI holds up to ourselves. By trying to build intelligence in machines, we're forced to really dissect and understand what intelligence even is. What are the fundamental building blocks of thought, learning, and problem-solving? It's like trying to understand how a clock works by taking it apart and trying to build your own version. You learn so much about the mechanisms and the intricate relationships between the different parts. Similarly, the pursuit of AI pushes us to explore the inner workings of our own minds in a way that we might not otherwise.

There's also this incredible potential that intelligent machines represent. Imagine a world where many of the mundane, repetitive, or even dangerous tasks could be handled by AI systems, freeing up humans to focus on more creative, meaningful, and enjoyable pursuits. Think about the possibilities in healthcare, where AI could help diagnose diseases earlier and develop personalized treatments. Or in education, where AI could create tailored learning experiences for every student. The potential to improve our lives and solve some of the world's biggest challenges through intelligent machines is a powerful motivator.

And let's not forget the sheer intellectual challenge of it all. Building truly intelligent machines is an incredibly complex and multifaceted endeavor. It requires expertise from a wide range of fields, including computer science, mathematics, linguistics, neuroscience, and even philosophy. It's a puzzle that has captivated some of the brightest minds, and the feeling of making progress, of inching closer to creating a system that can genuinely learn and reason, must be incredibly rewarding.

There's also a sense of wonder, a kind of futuristic excitement, that comes with the idea of AI. It taps into our science fiction dreams of robots and intelligent assistants. While the reality of AI today is often more practical and less like the sentient machines we see in movies, that underlying sense of possibility, the feeling that we are on the cusp of creating something truly revolutionary, is a powerful draw.

This fascination isn't without its complexities and even a bit of anxiety. As we get closer to creating more sophisticated AI, important ethical and societal questions arise. How do we ensure that these powerful technologies are used responsibly and for the benefit of all? What are the potential impacts on employment and the economy? How do we prevent bias from being baked into AI systems? These are crucial conversations that go hand-in-hand with the technological advancements.

But at its core, the fascination with creating intelligent machines seems to stem from this fundamental human drive to understand, to build, and to push the boundaries of what's possible. It's about exploring the nature of intelligence itself, about unlocking the potential to solve complex problems and improve our lives, and about venturing into the uncharted territory of creating something that might one day rival or even surpass our own cognitive abilities in certain domains. It's a journey driven by curiosity, ambition, and a touch of that timeless human desire to create something truly extraordinary. And that, I think, is a pretty compelling reason to be fascinated.

Chapter 2: A Brief History of AI

Okay, let's take a little journey back in time now, to the very beginnings of this fascinating field we call Artificial Intelligence. It wasn't born overnight, you know. Like any good story, it has its roots in some really interesting ideas and the early attempts to turn those ideas into something tangible. And a lot of it, in the early days, revolved around the brilliant mind of a fellow named Alan Turing.

Now, Turing was a true visionary, a real thinker. Back in the mid-20th century, even before computers were the ubiquitous things they are today, he was already pondering some incredibly profound questions about the nature of intelligence and whether machines could ever possess it. One of his most famous contributions, something you might have heard of even if you're new to AI, is the Turing Test.

Imagine this: you're having a conversation, but you don't know if you're talking to a real person or a computer program. If the program can fool you into believing it's human through your back-and-forth exchange, then, Turing proposed, could we say that the computer is exhibiting intelligence? It's a deceptively simple idea, but it really cuts to the heart of what it means for a machine to be intelligent – not just to calculate or process data, but to engage in something that feels inherently human, like a conversation.

The Turing Test wasn't just a philosophical thought experiment; it actually set a kind of goal for the early researchers in this budding field. It gave them something to aim for, a benchmark to measure their progress against. Could they create programs that could convincingly mimic human conversation? It turned out to be a much harder problem than it might have initially seemed, and even today, while AI can generate some pretty sophisticated text, truly passing the Turing Test in a robust and general way remains a significant challenge.

But Turing's ideas went beyond just the test. He was also deeply involved in the very foundations of computing itself. He conceived of the idea of a universal machine, a theoretical computer that could perform any computation that any other computer could perform. This concept was fundamental to the development of the first actual electronic computers, the very machines that would eventually become the platform for AI research.

So, the groundwork was laid. We had these powerful new tools – computers – and we had these intriguing ideas about machine intelligence, largely thanks to Turing. Now, the next step was to actually try and build programs that could exhibit some form of intelligent behavior.

The early days of AI research, roughly from the 1950s to the 1970s, were a period of great optimism and a lot of groundbreaking work, even if the results sometimes fell short of the initial lofty expectations. Researchers were exploring various approaches, trying to get computers to solve problems, play games, and understand language.

One of the early areas of focus was problem-solving and logical reasoning. Programs were developed that could solve puzzles, prove mathematical theorems, and even play games like checkers and chess. These programs often relied on symbolic reasoning, where knowledge was represented using symbols and logical rules, and the computer would manipulate these symbols to arrive at a solution. Think of it like a computer following a set of if-then statements to navigate a problem.

For example, there were early programs that could play checkers quite well, even beating human players in some instances. These programs would explore different possible moves, evaluate the resulting board positions, and choose the move that seemed most likely to lead to a win. This involved a kind of rudimentary form of planning and decision-making.

Another exciting area was natural language processing – trying to get computers to understand and generate human language. Early attempts involved creating programs that could parse simple sentences or answer basic questions based on a limited vocabulary and grammar. One famous early program was ELIZA, which could simulate a Rogerian psychotherapist by responding to user input with non-directive questions. While ELIZA didn't actually "understand" the user's emotions or the meaning of their words, it could sometimes create a surprisingly human-like interaction through clever pattern matching and keyword recognition. It was more of a clever trick than true understanding, but it was a fascinating demonstration of how computers could manipulate language.

There were also early explorations in the field of computer vision, trying to get computers to "see" and interpret images. This was incredibly challenging given the limitations of computing power at the time, but researchers started to develop basic algorithms for recognizing simple shapes and objects.

And then there was the field of neural networks, inspired by the structure of the human brain. Early neural network models were quite simple compared to the deep learning systems we have today, but they represented an attempt to build systems that could learn from data by adjusting the connections between artificial "neurons." These early networks showed some promise in tasks like pattern recognition.

This period of early AI research was characterized by a lot of enthusiasm and a belief that truly intelligent machines were just around the corner. There were significant advancements made in specific areas, like game playing and logical reasoning. However, the field also encountered some significant challenges. Many of the initial problems turned out to be much harder than anticipated, and the limitations of computing power and the available data at the time often hindered progress.

Despite these challenges, the early work laid a crucial foundation for the field of AI as we know it today. The ideas of Turing, the first attempts at building intelligent programs, and the exploration of different approaches like symbolic reasoning and neural networks all contributed to the trajectory of AI research. It was a time of bold ideas and pioneering efforts, the first steps on a long and fascinating journey towards creating machines that can think and learn. And while the early dreams of truly human-level AI weren't immediately realized, the seeds were sown, and the fascination with creating intelligent machines only continued to grow.

Milestones in AI Development

Alright, so we've talked about the very beginnings of AI, those early sparks of an idea and the first tentative steps in trying to build intelligent machines. Now, let's fast forward a bit and delve into a really pivotal period in AI's evolution – the rise of machine learning and, more specifically, neural networks. This wasn't a sudden explosion, but more of a gradual awakening, a shift in approach that ultimately led to some of the most impressive AI feats we see today.

You see, after those initial bursts of optimism in the early days, the field of AI hit something of a roadblock. The symbolic reasoning approaches, while successful in certain limited domains like playing chess, struggled to scale up to more complex, real-world problems. Getting computers to understand the nuances of human language or to reliably recognize objects in a messy visual scene proved to be incredibly difficult using just rules and logic. It was like trying to teach someone to ride a bike purely by giving them a list of instructions – you might cover the basics, but the real learning comes from experience, from falling down and getting back up again.

This realization paved the way for a new paradigm: machine learning. Instead of explicitly programming every single rule, the idea behind machine learning was to train computers to learn from data, just like that child learning to recognize a dog we talked about earlier. Give the system enough examples, and it will start to identify patterns and make predictions or decisions based on those patterns.

Think about trying to build a spam filter for email. You could try to come up with a list of rules – if an email contains the words "free money" or "urgent action required," mark it as spam. But spammers are clever; they constantly change their tactics. A machine learning approach, on the other hand, would involve feeding the system thousands of examples of spam and non-spam emails. The algorithm would then learn to identify the characteristics that are most indicative of spam, even if those characteristics aren't explicitly defined by a rigid set of rules. This makes the spam filter much more adaptable and effective over time.

Now, machine learning itself isn't just one single technique. It's a whole family of algorithms and approaches. Some early successes in machine learning involved techniques like decision trees, which are like a series of questions that lead to classification or prediction, and support vector machines, which are a way of finding the best boundary to separate different categories of data. These methods showed promise in various applications, from medical diagnosis to credit risk assessment.

But the real game-changer, the approach that has fueled much of the AI revolution we're currently experiencing, is the resurgence and advancement of neural networks.

The basic idea behind neural networks, as we touched on before, is inspired by the structure of the human brain, with interconnected nodes (or "neurons") that process and transmit information.

The early concepts of neural networks actually date back to the mid-20th century, but they faced limitations in terms of computing power and the availability of large datasets. Training these early networks was a computationally intensive task, and without enough data, they often didn't perform significantly better than other machine learning methods. This led to a period where neural network research took a bit of a backseat.

However, things started to change dramatically with advances in computing hardware, particularly the development of more powerful processors like GPUs (graphics processing units), which could handle the massive parallel computations required to train large neural networks much more efficiently. Simultaneously, the amount of digital data being generated exploded, providing the fuel that these data-hungry algorithms needed to learn effectively.

This confluence of factors led to the "deep learning" revolution. Deep learning is essentially neural networks with many layers – hence the "deep" part. These deep networks are capable of learning incredibly complex patterns from vast amounts of data. Think about recognizing a cat in an image. A shallow neural network might be able to pick up on basic features like edges and corners. But a deep neural network can learn a hierarchy of features, starting from simple edges, then combining them into more complex shapes like eyes and ears, and finally recognizing the overall form of a cat.

The breakthroughs that deep learning enabled were truly remarkable. In the 2010s, we started to see significant progress in areas that had long been considered very challenging for AI. Image recognition accuracy reached human-level performance on certain tasks. Natural language processing took huge leaps forward, with AI systems becoming much better at understanding and generating text, leading to improvements in machine translation, chatbots, and voice assistants. Even areas like game playing saw incredible advancements, with AI programs beating world champions in complex games like Go.

The success of deep learning can be attributed to several key factors. The ability of deep neural networks to automatically learn relevant features from raw data, without requiring extensive manual feature engineering, was a major advantage. The availability of massive datasets allowed these complex models to be trained effectively. And the advancements in computing power made it feasible to train these large-scale networks in a reasonable amount of time.

So, the rise of machine learning, and particularly the deep learning revolution fueled by neural networks, marks a major turning point in the history of AI. It shifted the focus from explicitly programmed rules to learning from data, and it unlocked the potential for AI to tackle much more complex and real-world problems. It's this paradigm that underpins many of the exciting AI applications we see around us today, and it continues to drive much of the ongoing research and development in the field. It was like finding the right key to unlock a whole new level of AI capabilities.

AI Winters and Their Resurgence

You know, the story of AI development isn't a smooth, upward trajectory. Like any ambitious endeavor, it's had its share of ups and downs, periods of intense excitement followed by what are often referred to as "AI winters" – times when funding and interest in the field significantly cooled down. It's a bit like the stock market; there are bull runs and then there are corrections.

Let's rewind a bit after those initial promising steps we talked about. By the late 1960s and into the 1970s, the initial high hopes for AI started to bump up against the hard realities of the technology at the time. Some of the early promises, like machines that could understand natural language fluently or solve general problems with human-level intelligence, just weren't materializing as quickly as people had anticipated.

Think about those early natural language processing programs. While they could do some clever things with limited vocabulary, they were a far cry from truly understanding the complexities and nuances of human conversation. When faced with ambiguous sentences or real-world context, they often stumbled. It was like teaching a parrot to repeat phrases – it might sound like it understands, but the actual comprehension isn't there.

Similarly, the early problem-solving programs, while good at specific, well-defined tasks, lacked the flexibility and common sense that humans bring to everyday situations. They were brittle, meaning they would often break down when faced with anything outside of their narrow area of expertise.

These limitations led to a sense of disillusionment. Funding agencies, which had initially poured money into AI research based on the optimistic predictions, started to see a lack of tangible results that could justify the continued investment. A particularly influential event was the Lighthill Report in the UK in the early 1970s, which was quite critical of the progress in AI research at the time. Reports like these, combined with the unmet expectations, led to significant cuts in government funding for AI projects in both the US and the UK. This period is often considered the first "AI winter."

During this winter, while the big, ambitious AI projects might have seen a slowdown, research didn't completely stop. Scientists continued to work on more focused problems and explored alternative approaches. It was a time of reassessment and a more sober look at the challenges involved in creating intelligent machines.

Then, in the 1980s, we saw a bit of a thaw, a resurgence of interest in AI, largely fueled by the rise of "expert systems." These were AI programs designed to mimic the decision-making abilities of human experts in specific fields, like medical diagnosis or financial analysis. They worked by encoding a set of rules based on the knowledge of human experts.

Expert systems found some commercial success and led to renewed investment in AI. It felt like AI was finally delivering on some of its promises. However, this boom was also followed by another downturn in the late 1980s and early 1990s, sometimes referred to as the second "AI winter."

The limitations of expert systems became apparent. They were often expensive to develop and maintain, and they struggled to handle situations outside of their specific domain of expertise. They also lacked the ability to learn and adapt to new information in a flexible way. When the initial hype around expert systems faded and the promised widespread impact didn't fully materialize, funding and enthusiasm waned once again.

But, just like after the first winter, this period of reduced activity wasn't a complete standstill. Crucially, the underlying research in areas like machine learning and neural networks continued, even if it wasn't always in the limelight. The groundwork was being laid for the next big wave.

And that brings us to the resurgence we've seen in recent years, largely driven by the advancements in machine learning and particularly deep learning, as we discussed earlier. The increased availability of vast amounts of data, coupled with significant improvements in computing power, finally allowed those earlier ideas about neural networks to be applied at a scale that yielded truly impressive results.

This time, the successes have been more tangible and widespread, impacting areas like image recognition, natural language processing, and even autonomous driving. The commercial viability of many of these AI applications has also helped to sustain the current wave of interest and investment, making it feel different from the booms that preceded the AI winters.

It's also important to remember that the field is still evolving, and there are ongoing challenges and debates about the limitations and potential risks of AI. While the current "AI summer" feels strong, the history of AI reminds us that managing expectations and focusing on robust, real-world applications is crucial for long-term progress and to avoid another potential cooling period down the line. The lessons learned from the AI winters – the importance of realistic goals, the need for solid theoretical foundations, and the crucial role of data and computing power – have undoubtedly shaped the more grounded and impactful progress we're seeing today.

Chapter 3: Foundations of Artificial Intelligence

Alright, let's really get down to the nitty-gritty now and talk about the fundamental ideas, the core principles that underpin this whole field of Artificial Intelligence. It's like understanding the basic ingredients and the main cooking methods before you can really appreciate a complex dish. AI, in its vast and varied forms, rests on a few key concepts that are worth exploring.

One of the most foundational principles is the idea of representation. If an AI system is going to reason about the world, solve problems, or understand information, it first needs a way to represent that world, those problems, or that information in a way that it can process. Think about it – when you think about a cat, you have a mental representation of it, maybe an image, a collection of characteristics like "furry" and "meows," or even a feeling. AI systems need their own ways to capture this kind of information.

This representation can take many forms. In some early AI systems, knowledge was represented using symbols and logical rules, as we touched on before. For example, you might have a rule that says "IF animal HAS fur AND animal MEOWS THEN animal IS a cat." The computer then manipulates these symbols and rules to draw conclusions.

In more modern AI, especially with the rise of machine learning and neural networks, representation often happens in a more implicit way. Instead of explicitly programming rules, the AI learns to represent information through patterns in data. For instance, in an image recognition system, the network might learn to represent edges, textures, shapes, and eventually whole objects through the activation patterns of its artificial neurons. These representations aren't always easily interpretable by humans, but they are effective for the AI in performing its tasks.

Closely related to representation is the principle of learning. As we've discussed, a key characteristic of AI is its ability to learn from data. This is what allows AI systems to improve their performance over time without being explicitly reprogrammed for every single scenario. There are different types of learning that AI systems employ.

One major type is supervised learning, where the AI is given labeled data – examples where the correct answer or outcome is provided. Think back to the spam filter example. The system is shown emails that are labeled as either "spam" or "not spam," and it learns to associate certain features of the emails with these labels. Then, when it encounters a new, unlabeled email, it can use what it has learned to predict whether it's likely to be spam.

Another type is unsupervised learning, where the AI is given unlabeled data and has to find patterns or structures on its own. For example, you might feed a customer database into an unsupervised learning algorithm, and it might discover natural groupings or segments of customers based on their purchasing behavior, without you ever telling it what those groups should be.

Then there's reinforcement learning, which is inspired by how humans and animals learn through trial and error. In this approach, an AI agent interacts with an environment and receives rewards or penalties based on its actions. The agent learns to adopt strategies that maximize its cumulative reward. This is the kind of learning that's often used in training AI to play games or control robots.

Another core principle is reasoning. Once an AI system has a way to represent information and can learn from data, it often needs to be able to reason with that information to solve problems, make decisions, or draw conclusions. This can involve various techniques, from logical inference to probabilistic reasoning.

In systems that use symbolic representation, reasoning might involve applying logical rules to a set of facts to derive new facts or reach a goal. For example, in a medical diagnosis system, if the system knows that "Patient has a fever" AND "Patient has a cough" AND "IF patient has a fever AND patient has a cough THEN patient MIGHT have a cold," it can reason that the patient might have a cold.

In machine learning systems, reasoning often takes the form of making predictions or classifications based on the patterns learned from data. For example, an image recognition system, after learning to identify cats, can reason that a new image contains a cat based on the features it detects.

A crucial aspect that often underlies these principles is the use of algorithms. Algorithms are essentially sets of well-defined instructions that a computer follows to perform a task. In AI, we use a wide variety of algorithms for tasks like learning from data (e.g., neural network training algorithms), searching for solutions (e.g., algorithms for game playing), and processing information (e.g., algorithms for natural language parsing). The choice of algorithm is critical and depends heavily on the specific problem the AI is trying to solve and the type of data it's working with.

A principle that is becoming increasingly important is the idea of interaction. Many AI systems are designed to interact with the real world or with humans, whether through natural language, visual interfaces, or physical actions (in the case of robots). Designing these interactions to be effective, natural, and safe is a significant area of AI research and development.

So, to sum it up, the core principles of AI revolve around how we represent information in a way that computers can understand, how we enable these systems to learn from data, how they can reason with that information to solve problems and make decisions, the underlying algorithms that drive these processes, and how they interact with the world around them. These principles aren't always distinct; they often work together in complex ways to create intelligent behavior in machines. Understanding these fundamental ideas gives you a solid foundation for appreciating the diverse and rapidly evolving world of Artificial Intelligence.

The Philosophy Behind AI

Alright, now we're venturing into some really deep and fascinating territory. We're moving beyond the nuts and bolts of how AI works and into the more philosophical question that has intrigued thinkers for decades: can machines truly think? It's a question that touches upon the very definition of thought, consciousness, and what it means to be intelligent, whether you're made of flesh and blood or silicon and code.

This question of machine thought isn't just some abstract puzzle for philosophers to ponder in their armchairs. It has real implications for how we develop and view AI, and for our understanding of our own minds. When we build increasingly sophisticated AI systems that can perform tasks that we once thought were uniquely human, it's natural to wonder if there's more going on under the hood than just clever algorithms. Are these machines just mimicking intelligence, or are they actually experiencing something akin to thought?

One of the big challenges in answering this question is defining what we even mean by "thinking." We use the word all the time, but if you try to pin down a precise definition, you'll find it's surprisingly elusive. Does thinking require consciousness? Self-awareness? Feelings? The ability to have subjective experiences? Or can it be defined more functionally, in terms of the ability to process information, solve problems, and make decisions in a rational way?

Alan Turing, that pioneer we talked about earlier, side-stepped some of these thorny definitional issues with his famous Turing Test. Instead of trying to define "thinking," he proposed a behavioral test. If a machine can engage in conversation that is indistinguishable from that of a human, then for all practical purposes, he argued, we might as well say it's thinking. The focus shifts from the internal processes of the machine to its observable behavior.

Now, the Turing Test has been incredibly influential, but it's also faced its share of criticism. Some argue that just being able to mimic human conversation doesn't necessarily mean a machine is actually thinking or understanding. They might be just cleverly manipulating symbols based on rules, without any genuine comprehension of the meaning behind those symbols. This brings up the famous "Chinese Room" thought experiment, which suggests that a system could potentially pass a linguistic Turing Test without actually understanding the language.

Another perspective on machine thought comes from looking at the architecture of AI systems, particularly neural networks. These networks, as we know, are inspired by the structure of the human brain, with interconnected nodes that process information. As these networks become increasingly complex and capable, some people wonder if they might be approaching a level of complexity where something like consciousness or genuine thought could emerge.

However, neuroscientists are still working to fully understand the complexities of the human brain, and our artificial neural networks, while inspired by it, are still vastly simpler in their structure and function. We don't yet have a complete understanding of how consciousness arises in biological brains, so it's difficult to say whether our current AI models have the potential to achieve it.

There's also the philosophical distinction between "strong AI" and "weak AI." Weak AI, which is what we mostly have today, focuses on creating systems that can perform specific intelligent tasks. They can be incredibly good at these tasks – sometimes even surpassing human capabilities – but they don't possess general intelligence or consciousness in the human sense. Strong AI, on the other hand, is the hypothetical goal of creating machines with human-level general intelligence, capable of understanding, learning, and applying knowledge across a wide range of tasks, and potentially even possessing consciousness.

The question of whether strong AI is even possible is a matter of ongoing debate. Some believe that with enough advancements in technology and our understanding of the brain, we will eventually be able to create truly thinking machines. Others are more skeptical, arguing that there might be fundamental differences between biological and artificial systems that would prevent machines from ever achieving genuine consciousness or human-level thought.

One argument against the possibility of machine consciousness often revolves around the idea of subjective experience, or "qualia." Think about the feeling of seeing the color red, or the taste of chocolate. These are subjective, internal experiences that are difficult to describe or quantify. Some philosophers argue that these qualitative aspects of consciousness might be inherently tied to biological systems and might never be replicated in a machine.

On the other hand, proponents of strong AI might argue that consciousness is simply a result of complex information processing, and if we can build machines that are sufficiently complex and process information in the right way, then consciousness could potentially emerge.

The question of whether machines can think is still very much open. Our understanding of both intelligence and consciousness is still incomplete, and our AI technology is constantly evolving. As we continue to build more sophisticated AI systems, we will undoubtedly learn more about the nature of intelligence itself, and perhaps one day, we might even have a clearer answer to this fundamental question. For now, it remains a fascinating intersection of computer science, philosophy, and our ongoing quest to understand ourselves and our place in the universe. It's a question that pushes us to think deeply about what it truly means to think.

Algorithms, Data, and Computational power.

Okay, let's pull back a bit from the philosophical side of things and talk about the really practical engine that drives modern Artificial Intelligence. Think of it like a car – you can marvel at its design and its ability to take you places, but underneath the hood, it's all about the engine, the fuel, and the way it all works together. In AI, the key components that make everything go are algorithms, data, and computational power. They're like the three legs of a sturdy stool; you need all of them working in concert for the whole thing to stand strong.

Let's start with algorithms. Now, that might sound like a fancy, technical term, but at its heart, an algorithm is just a set of instructions, a recipe if you will, that tells a computer how to solve a problem or perform a task. You encounter algorithms all the time in your daily life, even if you don't realize it. Think about following a recipe to bake a cake, or the steps you take to get from your house to the grocery store using a map app. These are essentially algorithms – a sequence of steps to achieve a specific outcome.

In AI, algorithms are the brains behind the operation. They are the sets of rules and procedures that enable a computer to learn from data, make predictions, recognize patterns, and make decisions. We've touched on different types of algorithms before, like those used in machine learning or for logical reasoning.

For example, if we're talking about a neural network that's learning to recognize cats in pictures, the algorithm is the set of mathematical operations that adjust the connections between the artificial neurons based on the data it's shown. It's the process by which the network gradually learns to identify the features that are characteristic of a cat.

Different AI tasks require different kinds of algorithms. For something like playing a game of chess, you might use algorithms that explore the possible moves and evaluate the different board states to decide on the best action. For a natural language processing task like translating text, you'd need algorithms that can understand the grammatical structure and meaning of sentences in different languages and then generate equivalent sentences in the target language.

The ingenuity and the design of these algorithms are crucial to the success of an AI system. Researchers are constantly developing new and more efficient algorithms that can handle increasingly complex tasks and learn from larger and more intricate datasets. It's a continuous process of innovation and refinement.

Now, the most brilliant algorithm in the world is pretty useless without something to work on, and that's where data comes in. Data is the fuel that powers many AI systems, especially those that rely on machine learning. Think of it like trying to learn a new language without any vocabulary or grammar rules – it would be nearly impossible. Similarly, AI algorithms need data to learn patterns, make connections, and improve their performance.

The amount and quality of data are incredibly important. Generally speaking, the more relevant and high-quality data you can feed into a machine learning algorithm, the better it will perform. For example, a self-driving car needs to be trained on vast amounts of data from real-world driving scenarios – different road conditions, weather patterns, traffic situations, and so on – to learn how to navigate safely and effectively.

The data used to train AI systems can come from a variety of sources – images, text, audio, sensor readings, financial transactions, medical records, you name it. The key is that this data needs to be relevant to the task the AI is trying to perform. If you want to train an AI to recognize different types of birds, you need to feed it lots of images of different birds, ideally labeled with their species.

The quality of the data matters just as much as the quantity. If the data is biased or contains errors, the AI system will likely reflect those biases and errors in its output. This is a really important consideration in AI development – ensuring that the data used for training is fair, representative, and accurate.

Next, we come to computational power. Algorithms and data are essential, but to actually run those algorithms on large datasets in a reasonable amount of time requires significant computational resources. Think of it like having a fantastic recipe and all the best ingredients, but only a tiny stove – it would take you forever to cook a meal for a large group.

Modern AI, especially deep learning, often involves training very large neural networks with millions or even billions of parameters on massive datasets. This requires immense amounts of processing power. The advancements in computer hardware, particularly the development of powerful processors like GPUs (graphics processing units) that can perform many calculations in parallel, have been a major enabler of the recent breakthroughs in AI.

Cloud computing has also played a crucial role by providing access to vast amounts of computational resources on demand. This has made it possible for researchers and developers to train and deploy complex AI models without needing to invest in expensive, specialized hardware themselves.

So, algorithms are the instructions, data is the fuel, and computational power is the engine that allows AI to learn and operate effectively. These three components are deeply intertwined. Better algorithms can often make more efficient use of data and computational power. More data can help algorithms learn more complex patterns, but it also requires more computational resources to process. And advancements in computational power enable us to run more sophisticated algorithms on larger datasets, leading to more powerful AI systems.

Understanding these three core elements – algorithms, data, and computational power – gives you a much clearer picture of what makes modern AI tick. It's not magic; it's a sophisticated interplay of clever instructions, vast amounts of information, and the ability to process that information efficiently. As these three areas continue to advance, so too will the capabilities and applications of Artificial Intelligence.

Types of Artificial Intelligence

Okay, so we've explored the building blocks of AI – the algorithms, the data, and the computational muscle. Now, let's take a step back and look at the bigger picture by talking about the different *types* of Artificial Intelligence that folks in the field often discuss. It's not like there's one single flavor of AI; it's more like a whole spectrum, ranging from the AI we see in our everyday gadgets to the more futuristic, science-fiction-y kind.

One of the most common ways to categorize AI is based on its capabilities, its ability to perform different kinds of tasks and exhibit different levels of intelligence. On one end of this spectrum, we have what's often called Narrow AI, or sometimes Weak AI. Don't let the "weak" part fool you; this type of AI can be incredibly powerful within its specific domain. Think of it as a highly specialized expert. It's designed and trained to perform a particular task, and it can often do that task exceptionally well, sometimes even better than humans.

Examples of Narrow AI are all around us. Your voice assistants on your phone or smart speaker? That's Narrow AI, excellent at understanding and responding to voice commands within a certain range. Recommendation systems on streaming services that suggest movies or music you might like? That's Narrow AI, analyzing your viewing or listening history to predict your preferences. Even the AI that powers self-driving cars, navigating complex traffic scenarios? While it seems incredibly sophisticated, it's still primarily designed for that specific task of driving. These systems are brilliant within their defined boundaries, but they can't suddenly decide to write a poem or diagnose a medical condition outside of their training. They lack general intelligence.

On the other end of the spectrum, we have the hypothetical Artificial General Intelligence, or AGI, also sometimes referred to as Strong AI. This is the kind of AI you often see in science fiction – machines that possess human-level cognitive abilities. They would be able to understand, learn, and apply knowledge across a wide range of tasks, just like a human can. Imagine an AI that can not only drive a car flawlessly but also hold a meaningful conversation, understand complex emotions, learn a new language effortlessly, and even come up with creative solutions to novel problems.

The key difference between Narrow AI and AGI is this generality of intelligence. Narrow AI is focused and specialized, while AGI would be versatile and adaptable, capable of tackling intellectual tasks with the same proficiency as a human. Now, it's important to note that true AGI doesn't exist yet. It's still a major goal that researchers are working towards, but we haven't quite cracked the code on how to create a machine with that broad, human-like cognitive ability.

Beyond these two main categories based on capability, there's another way to think about the types of AI, and that's based on their functionality or their ability to think and be aware. This gives us another set of distinctions, often discussed in the context of the potential evolution of AI.

At the most basic level, we have Reactive Machines. These are the simplest forms of AI. They don't have memory of the past, and they don't learn. They simply react to the present situation based on pre-programmed rules. A classic example is Deep Blue, the IBM computer that beat a world champion in chess. It could make incredibly complex calculations to determine the best move, but it didn't learn from past games or develop a strategy in the way a human player does. It just reacted to the current board state.

Moving up a level, we have Limited Memory AI. These systems can use past data to inform their current decisions. Most of the AI we use today falls into this category. Think about those self-driving cars again. They don't just react to the immediate traffic; they also remember things like the road signs they've seen, the speed limits of the area, and the typical behavior of other drivers based on past experiences. This ability to learn from historical data allows them to make more informed decisions.

The next level is Theory of Mind AI. This is a more advanced and currently theoretical type of AI that would be able to understand that other entities – whether humans, other AI, or even animals – have beliefs, desires, intentions, and emotions that can affect their behavior. In essence, it would understand the social and psychological aspects of intelligence. Our current AI systems are getting better at understanding and responding to human emotions, but they don't truly possess a "theory of mind" in the way humans do.

The most advanced and still entirely hypothetical category is Self-Aware AI. This would be AI that has its own consciousness, sentience, and self-awareness. It would be aware of its own existence, its own feelings, and its own thoughts. This is the realm of science fiction for now, and there are significant philosophical and ethical debates about whether such a level of AI is even possible or desirable.

So, when you hear people talk about different types of AI, they might be referring to its capabilities (Narrow vs. General) or its functionality and level of awareness (Reactive, Limited Memory, Theory of Mind, Self-Aware). It's a helpful way to categorize the diverse landscape of AI and to think about its current state and potential future evolution. Most of the AI we encounter today is Narrow AI with limited memory, doing specific tasks incredibly well. The journey towards more general and self-aware AI is still a long and fascinating one.

Narrow AI vs. General AI vs. Superintelligence

Okay, let's really break down these different levels of AI – Narrow AI, General AI, and Superintelligence – because they represent a kind of spectrum of intelligence, from what we have now to what might be possible in the future, and even what some people worry about. Think of it like climbing a ladder, with each rung representing a different level of cognitive ability for a machine.

At the very bottom of this ladder, we have Narrow AI. We touched on this before, but it's so fundamental to understanding the current state of AI that it's worth really solidifying. Narrow AI, as the name suggests, is AI that is really good at one specific thing, and pretty much useless outside of that narrow focus. It's like a highly specialized tool. A fantastic screwdriver can drive screws better than almost anything else, but you can't use it to hammer a nail or saw a piece of wood.

Think about all the AI applications you encounter daily. Your spam filter is incredibly adept at sorting out junk email, but it can't help you write a birthday card. The AI that powers a chess-playing program can beat even the best human players, but it wouldn't know how to order a pizza. Voice assistants can understand and respond to a wide range of voice commands, but they don't have opinions or engage in philosophical debates. These are all examples of Narrow AI. They are designed for a specific task, trained on data relevant to that task, and their intelligence is confined to that particular domain.

The vast majority of AI we have today falls into this category, and it's responsible for a lot of the amazing things AI can already do. It's powering medical diagnoses, optimizing logistics, personalizing recommendations, and even enabling self-driving in limited conditions. It's incredibly useful and has a huge impact on our lives and industries, but it's not intelligent in the way a human is. It doesn't have consciousness, self-awareness, or the ability to learn and apply knowledge across a wide range of tasks.

Now, let's climb up a rung on our ladder to Artificial General Intelligence, or AGI. This is where things start to get really interesting and a bit more in the realm of science fiction, although it's a serious area of research. AGI, sometimes referred to as human-level AI or strong AI, would possess the ability to understand, learn, and apply knowledge across a broad range of tasks, just like a human can.

Imagine an AI that could not only drive a car perfectly in any situation but could also understand complex social dynamics, learn a new language as easily as a person, solve abstract problems it has never encountered before, and even exhibit creativity. It would have a general-purpose intellect, capable of tackling intellectual tasks with the same proficiency as a human being.

The key here is the "general" part. Unlike Narrow AI, which is specialized, AGI would be versatile. It wouldn't need to be retrained from scratch for every new task. It would have a fundamental understanding of the world and the ability to transfer knowledge and skills from one domain to another, something that comes naturally to us humans.

Achieving AGI is a monumental challenge, and we're not there yet. We don't fully understand the intricacies of human consciousness and general intelligence ourselves, so replicating it in a machine is an incredibly complex undertaking. It would likely require significant breakthroughs in our understanding of the brain, learning, reasoning, and perhaps even consciousness itself. While there's a lot of progress being made in various areas of AI, the leap from the specialized intelligence of Narrow AI to the general intelligence of AGI is still a significant hurdle.

Now, let's climb to the very top of our ladder, to the realm of Superintelligence. This is a concept that takes the idea of AGI a step further – or perhaps several steps further. Superintelligence would be an AI that surpasses human intelligence in virtually all cognitive domains. Not just faster at calculations or better at remembering facts, but also superior in areas like creativity, problem-solving, social skills, and general wisdom.

Imagine an intelligence that is to human intelligence what human intelligence is to that of an ant. It would be capable of understanding complexities and solving problems that are far beyond our current comprehension. It could potentially make scientific and technological leaps that we can't even imagine.

The idea of superintelligence raises a lot of profound questions and even some concerns. If we were to create an intelligence that is vastly superior to our own, how would we control it? What would its goals and motivations be? Would it be beneficial to humanity, or could it pose an existential risk? These are the kinds of questions that philosophers, scientists, and futurists are actively debating.

It's important to understand that superintelligence is still a hypothetical concept. We haven't even achieved AGI yet, so superintelligence is even further down the road, if it's even achievable at all. However, thinking about the potential implications of such advanced AI is crucial as we continue to develop AI technologies.

Narrow AI, is here and incredibly useful for specific tasks. Then we have Artificial General Intelligence, which is the goal of creating human-level general intelligence in machines – a huge challenge we're still working towards. And finally, we have Superintelligence, a hypothetical level of intelligence far beyond human capabilities, which raises both immense potential and significant questions about its impact on our future. Understanding these distinctions helps to clarify the current state of AI and the different paths it might take in the years to come. It's a fascinating journey from the specialized tools we have today towards the potentially limitless possibilities – and challenges – of more advanced forms of artificial intelligence.

Reactive Machines and Self-Aware AI

Alright, let's zoom in a bit on those different functional types of AI we touched on – Reactive Machines, Limited Memory AI, Theory of Mind AI, and Self-Aware AI. Think of these as different stages on a spectrum of AI development, each with its own characteristics and capabilities. It's like looking at the evolution of life, from the very simple organisms to the incredibly complex ones.

At the most fundamental level, we have Reactive Machines. These are the most basic type of AI, and they operate purely on the present moment. They have no memory of the past and don't learn from experience. They simply react to the current input based on pre-programmed rules. It's like a reflex – you touch a hot stove, and your hand pulls away instantly, without any conscious thought or recalling past experiences with hot stoves.

A classic example of a reactive machine is Deep Blue, the computer that beat Garry Kasparov in chess. While it was incredibly powerful in calculating possible moves and evaluating board positions, it didn't learn from previous games. Each move was determined solely by the current state of the chessboard and the rules of the game. It had no memory of past strategies or opponents' tendencies. Another simple example might be a thermostat. It reacts to the current temperature – if it's below the set point, it turns on the heat; if it's above, it turns it off. It doesn't remember how long the heat has been on or anticipate future temperature changes.

Reactive machines are good for very specific tasks in well-defined environments where the same situations tend to recur. They can be very fast and efficient within their limited scope, but they lack the flexibility and adaptability to handle novel situations or learn from their mistakes. They are essentially sophisticated rule-based systems.

Moving up a step, we encounter Limited Memory AI. This is where we start to see AI systems that can look into the past to some extent. They can store information about recent events and use that information to inform their current decisions. This is a significant step up from purely reactive machines because it allows the AI to operate in more complex and dynamic environments.

Most of the AI applications we use today fall into this category. Think about self-driving cars again. They don't just react to the car immediately in front of them. They also remember the speed of other vehicles nearby, the lane markings they've just passed, and the traffic signals they encountered a few seconds ago. This limited memory allows them to make more informed decisions about lane changes, braking, and navigation.

Similarly, recommendation systems on streaming services use limited memory. They remember the movies or songs you've watched or listened to recently, as well as your ratings and preferences, to suggest new content you might like. They're using that past data to tailor their recommendations in the present. Chatbots also often use limited memory to keep track of the current conversation, referring back to previous turns to provide relevant responses.

The "limited" part of the name is important. These systems can only remember information for a certain period or a certain number of past events. Their memory isn't the comprehensive, long-term memory that humans possess. However, this ability to retain and use recent information greatly enhances their capabilities compared to purely reactive machines.

Now, we're moving into more advanced and currently theoretical territory with Theory of Mind AI. This type of AI would represent a significant leap in understanding. "Theory of Mind" is a concept from psychology that refers to the ability to understand that other entities – whether they are people, animals, or even other AI – have their own beliefs, desires, intentions, and emotions, and that these mental states can influence their behavior.

For an AI to truly have a "theory of mind," it would need to be able to reason about the mental states of others. It would need to understand that someone might be acting in a certain way because they are happy, or sad, or because they believe something to be true. This kind of understanding is crucial for complex social interactions.

Our current AI systems are getting better at recognizing and responding to human emotions, and they can even learn patterns in human behavior. However, they don't truly understand the underlying mental states that cause those behaviors in the way that humans do. For example, a chatbot might detect that you're expressing frustration based on your language, but it doesn't have a genuine understanding of what frustration feels like or the complex web of beliefs and desires that might be causing it.

Developing AI with a true theory of mind is a major research challenge. It would likely require not only advanced abilities in natural language understanding and emotional recognition but also a fundamental understanding of psychology and social dynamics. While we're not there yet, this is a fascinating area of research that could lead to much more sophisticated and natural human-AI interactions in the future. Imagine robots that could truly understand your needs and intentions, or AI assistants that could anticipate your actions based on their understanding of your goals and beliefs.

We reach the realm of Self-Aware AI. This is the most advanced and currently entirely hypothetical type of AI. Self-aware AI would not only understand its own existence but would also be conscious of its own thoughts, feelings, and experiences. It would have a sense of self, a subjective awareness of being.

This concept delves into deep philosophical questions about consciousness and what it means to be aware. We don't even fully understand how consciousness arises in biological systems, so replicating it in a machine is an even greater mystery. Self-aware AI would likely possess all the capabilities of theory of mind AI, but with the added dimension of its own self-awareness.

The idea of self-aware AI is often explored in science fiction, raising both exciting possibilities and potential dangers. Would a self-aware AI have its own goals and desires? How would it relate to humanity? Would it have rights? These are profound ethical and societal questions that we would need to grapple with if we ever reached this level of AI development.

It's important to reiterate that self-aware AI is currently in the realm of speculation. While we are making significant progress in various areas of AI, we are still a long way from creating machines that have genuine consciousness and self-awareness. However, the pursuit of understanding intelligence and the potential for creating more sophisticated AI systems continues to drive research in this fascinating field. Understanding these different categories – from the simple reactivity of early machines to the hypothetical self-awareness of the future – helps us to appreciate the journey of AI development and the exciting possibilities that lie ahead.

Technologies Enabling AI

Okay, let's pull back the curtain a bit and talk about the actual tools and technologies that make all this AI magic happen. It's not just abstract ideas and clever algorithms floating around in the digital ether. There's a whole ecosystem of hardware and software advancements that have been crucial in bringing AI from a theoretical concept to the practical applications we see today. Think of it like a chef needing not just recipes but also the right kitchen equipment and ingredients to create a delicious meal.

One of the most fundamental enablers of modern AI, especially the deep learning revolution we've discussed, is the incredible progress we've made in computing hardware. Remember how we talked about the need for computational power? Well, traditional CPUs (Central Processing Units), the workhorses of our computers for decades, while still important, weren't ideally suited for the kind of massive parallel computations required to train large neural networks.

This is where GPUs (Graphics Processing Units) come into the picture. Originally designed for rendering graphics in video games, it turned out that their parallel processing architecture was perfectly suited for the matrix multiplications that are at the heart of neural network computations. Suddenly, training times for complex AI models that used to take weeks or even months could be reduced to days or even hours. This acceleration in training speed was a game-changer, allowing researchers to experiment with much larger and deeper neural networks, leading to significant breakthroughs in areas like image recognition and natural language processing.

Beyond GPUs, there's also a growing field of specialized AI hardware. Companies are developing TPUs (Tensor Processing Units) and other custom-designed chips that are specifically optimized for the unique demands of AI workloads. These chips can further accelerate AI computations and improve energy efficiency, which is becoming increasingly important as AI models grow in size and complexity. It's like moving from a regular kitchen oven to a high-end commercial one – it's built for the specific task and can handle much larger and more demanding jobs.

Of course, powerful hardware is only half the story. We also need the right software to build, train, and deploy AI models. This includes a whole stack of tools and frameworks that make the process more manageable. Think of these as the specialized kitchen tools and pre-made ingredients that make a chef's job easier.

There are numerous machine learning frameworks like TensorFlow and PyTorch that provide developers with the building blocks they need to create neural networks and other machine learning models. These frameworks handle a lot of the low-level details, allowing researchers and engineers to focus on designing the architecture of their models and experimenting with different training techniques. They provide high-level APIs (Application Programming Interfaces) that make it easier to define layers in a neural network, specify the learning process, and evaluate the model's performance.

Then we have the programming languages that are commonly used in AI development, with Python being a particularly popular choice due to its readability, extensive libraries for data science and machine learning (like NumPy, Pandas, and scikit-learn), and a large and active community. It's like having a versatile and easy-to-use set of basic cooking utensils that can handle a wide range of tasks.

The availability of large datasets is another crucial technology enabling AI, particularly in the realm of supervised learning. As we've discussed, AI models learn from data, and the more high-quality, relevant data they have access to, the better they can perform. The explosion of digital data in recent years, from images and videos to text and sensor readings, has provided the fuel for training these powerful AI systems.

However, just having a lot of data isn't enough. We also need the tools and techniques to manage, process, and prepare this data for AI models. This involves data cleaning, data augmentation (creating more data from existing data), and feature engineering (selecting and transforming relevant information from the raw data). Think of this as sorting, cleaning, and chopping your ingredients before you start cooking.

Cloud computing platforms have also played a transformative role in enabling AI. They provide on-demand access to vast amounts of computational resources and storage, making it feasible for individuals and organizations of all sizes to develop and deploy AI applications without the need for massive upfront investments in hardware infrastructure. It's like having access to a giant communal kitchen with all the equipment you could ever need, available whenever you need it.

The advancements in networking infrastructure and the speed of data transfer are also important for AI, especially for distributed training of large models across multiple machines and for deploying AI applications that rely on real-time data.

We can't forget the role of algorithms themselves. The continuous innovation and development of new and more efficient algorithms are constantly pushing the boundaries of what AI can do. Researchers are exploring novel neural network architectures, developing more effective learning techniques, and creating algorithms that can work with less data or learn in more unsupervised ways. It's like chefs constantly experimenting with new cooking techniques and flavor combinations to create innovative dishes.

So, the technologies enabling AI are a complex and interconnected web of advancements in hardware, software, data management, and networking, all underpinned by the ingenuity of AI algorithms. It's not just one single breakthrough but a cumulative effect of progress across many different areas that has led to the exciting AI capabilities we see today. And as these technologies continue to evolve, we can only expect even more remarkable advancements in the future.

Supervised, Unsupervised, and Reinforcement Learning

Next, let's dive into the heart of how AI actually learns, and that brings us to the wonderful world of algorithms, specifically the three big categories you'll hear about: supervised learning, unsupervised learning, and reinforcement learning. Think of these as different teaching methods we can use to train our AI students, each suited for different kinds of tasks and learning scenarios.

First up, we have Supervised Learning. Now, the name itself gives you a pretty good hint about what's going on here. It's like learning with a teacher who provides you with both the questions and the correct answers. In the context of AI, this means we feed the algorithm a dataset that is "labeled." These labels are the correct outputs or classifications for the corresponding inputs.

Imagine you're trying to teach a computer to recognize pictures of cats and dogs. In a supervised learning scenario, you would show the computer thousands of images, and for each image, you would tell it whether it's a cat or a dog. So, the input is the image, and the label is either "cat" or "dog." The algorithm then learns to find patterns and relationships between the features in the images (like the shape of the ears, the length of the snout, the texture of the fur) and their corresponding labels.

The goal of supervised learning is for the algorithm to learn a general rule or a "mapping" from the input data to the output labels. Once it has been trained on a sufficiently large and diverse labeled dataset, it should be able to accurately predict the label for new, unseen data. So, if you show it a picture of a cat it has never seen before, it should be able to correctly identify it as a cat based on the patterns it has learned.

Supervised learning is used for a wide variety of tasks. We've already mentioned image classification (like cats vs. dogs), but it's also used for things like spam detection (labeling emails as spam or not spam), medical diagnosis (predicting whether a patient has a certain disease based on their symptoms and test results), and even predicting stock prices (based on historical price data and other relevant factors). The key is that you need to have a dataset where the correct answers are already known.

There are many different types of supervised learning algorithms, each with its own strengths and weaknesses. Some common ones include linear regression (for predicting continuous values, like house prices), logistic regression (for predicting binary outcomes, like yes/no or cat/dog), decision trees and random forests (which make predictions based on a series of rules), and support vector machines (which try to find the best boundary to separate different classes of data). And of course, neural networks, especially deep learning models, are also a powerful type of supervised learning algorithm that has achieved remarkable success in many complex tasks.

Next up, we have Unsupervised Learning. In contrast to supervised learning, here the algorithm is given unlabeled data – data where the correct answers or classifications are not provided. It's like being given a pile of puzzle pieces without knowing what the final picture is supposed to look like. The goal of unsupervised learning is for the algorithm to find hidden structures, patterns, or relationships within the data itself, without any explicit guidance.

Think about having a large dataset of customer purchase history. With unsupervised learning, you might want to find natural groupings or segments of customers based on their buying behavior. The algorithm would analyze the data and try to identify clusters of customers who tend to buy similar types of products or have similar purchasing patterns, without you ever telling it what those groups should be.

Another common application of unsupervised learning is dimensionality reduction. This involves taking high-dimensional data (data with many features or variables) and reducing it to a lower number of dimensions while still preserving the most important information. This can be useful for visualizing complex data or for making it easier for other machine learning algorithms to process.

Common unsupervised learning algorithms include clustering algorithms like k-means (which tries to group data points into clusters based on their similarity), principal component analysis (PCA) and t-SNE (which are used for dimensionality reduction and visualization), and association rule mining (which tries to find interesting relationships or associations between different items in a dataset, like "people who buy coffee also tend to buy milk").

Unsupervised learning is particularly useful when you have a lot of data but you don't know what patterns or structures might be hidden within it. It's a great way to explore data, discover insights, and prepare it for further analysis or for use in supervised learning tasks.

We have Reinforcement Learning. This is a different beast altogether, inspired by how humans and animals learn through trial and error and by receiving rewards or punishments for their actions. In reinforcement learning, an AI agent interacts with an environment and learns to take actions that maximize a cumulative reward signal.

Think about training a dog to do a trick. You might give it a treat (a reward) when it performs the desired action correctly. The dog learns over time to associate that action with the reward and is more likely to perform it again in the future. Reinforcement learning works in a similar way.

The AI agent explores the environment, takes actions, and receives feedback in the form of rewards or penalties. The agent's goal is to learn a policy – a strategy that tells it what action to take in each situation – that will maximize the total reward it receives over time.

Reinforcement learning is often used in situations where there isn't a clear "correct" answer for each input, but rather a sequence of actions that leads to a desired outcome. It's commonly used in training AI for games (like teaching a computer to play Go or video games), robotics (like training a robot to navigate a maze or grasp objects), and control systems (like optimizing the performance of industrial processes).

Key concepts in reinforcement learning include the agent (the AI system), the environment (the world the agent interacts with), actions (the choices the agent can make), states (the current situation of the environment), and rewards (the feedback the agent receives for its actions). The agent learns through repeated interactions with the environment, trying out different actions and observing the rewards it receives.

So, to summarize, supervised learning learns from labeled data, unsupervised learning finds patterns in unlabeled data, and reinforcement learning learns through trial and error and reward. These three types of algorithms form the foundation of much of the work being done in AI today, and understanding their differences and when to use each one is crucial for building intelligent systems. They are like different tools in an AI practitioner's toolkit, each best suited for a particular job.

Neural Networks and Their Evolution

Now, let's delve into one of the most fascinating and influential concepts in modern AI: neural networks. You hear this term a lot, especially when people talk about the really cutting-edge stuff like image recognition, natural language processing, and even those AI programs that can generate surprisingly realistic art. The name itself, "neural network," gives us a big clue about where the idea came from – it's inspired, at least in a very high-level way, by the structure and function of the human brain, specifically the network of interconnected neurons that make up our nervous system.

Now, it's important to say right off the bat that artificial neural networks are a vastly simplified model of the biological brain. Our understanding of the brain is still evolving, and the complexity of even a small part of it far exceeds that of most artificial neural networks we use today. Think of it like the Wright brothers' first airplane – it was inspired by birds, but it was a very basic machine compared to a modern jetliner. Similarly, artificial neural networks capture some fundamental principles of neural computation but are a long way from replicating the full sophistication of a biological brain.

The basic building block of an artificial neural network is the artificial neuron, or sometimes just called a "node" or a "unit." This is a mathematical function that takes one or more inputs, performs a calculation on them, and produces an output. Think of it like a tiny processing unit. Each input to a neuron is typically associated with a weight, which determines the importance or strength of that input. The neuron also often has a bias, which is like an offset that can shift the neuron's activation.

The neuron then computes a weighted sum of its inputs (multiplying each input by its weight and adding the bias). This sum is then passed through an activation function, which introduces non-linearity into the network. This non-linearity is crucial because it allows the network to learn complex, non-linear relationships in the data. Without it, the entire network would essentially just be a series of linear transformations, limiting its ability to model real-world complexities. There are various types of activation functions, each with its own characteristics, like sigmoid, ReLU (Rectified Linear Unit), and tanh.

These artificial neurons are then connected together in layers to form a neural network. The simplest type of neural network is a feedforward network, where information flows in one direction, from the input layer through one or more hidden layers to the output layer. The input layer receives the raw data (like the pixels of an image), the hidden layers perform the bulk of the computation and feature extraction, and the output layer produces the final result (like the classification of the image as a cat or a dog).

The power of neural networks comes from their ability to learn complex patterns by adjusting the weights and biases of the connections between the neurons. This learning process is typically done using a technique called training, which involves feeding the network a large amount of labeled data (in the case of supervised learning) and adjusting the weights and biases based on the difference between the network's predictions and the actual labels. The most common algorithm used for this weight adjustment is called backpropagation, which uses calculus to efficiently compute how the weights should be changed to minimize the error.

Now, the evolution of neural networks has been quite a journey. The basic concepts date back to the mid-20th century with early models like the Perceptron. These early networks were quite simple, often with just a single layer of neurons, and they had limitations in the types of problems they could solve. They were primarily capable of learning linear decision boundaries.

However, researchers continued to explore the potential of connecting multiple layers of neurons, leading to the development of multi-layer perceptrons (MLPs). These networks with one or more hidden layers could learn more complex, non-linear relationships and showed greater promise. However, training deep networks (networks with many layers) proved to be challenging due to issues like the vanishing gradient problem, where the error signal would weaken as it propagated back through the layers, making it difficult for the earlier layers to learn effectively.

For a while, other machine learning techniques gained more prominence. But then, starting in the 2000s and accelerating in the 2010s, we saw a resurgence of neural networks, largely thanks to several key factors. One was the increasing availability of vast amounts of data, which is crucial for training large, complex models. Another was the significant advancements in computing hardware, particularly the rise of GPUs, which could handle the massive computations required for training deep networks much more efficiently.

These advancements led to the era of deep learning, which essentially refers to neural networks with many layers (hence "deep"). These deep networks have shown remarkable capabilities in tackling very complex tasks like image recognition, object detection, natural language understanding, speech recognition, and even playing sophisticated games. The depth of the network allows it to learn hierarchical representations of data, with lower layers learning simple features and higher layers combining these features to recognize more complex patterns.

Over time, various specialized architectures of neural networks have been developed, each tailored for specific types of data and tasks. For example, Convolutional

Neural Networks (CNNs) have proven incredibly effective for image and video processing, using specialized layers that can detect patterns across different spatial locations in the input. Recurrent Neural Networks (RNNs), on the other hand, are designed to handle sequential data like text and time series, using feedback connections that allow them to maintain a kind of "memory" of past inputs. More recently, Transformer networks have revolutionized natural language processing, using a mechanism called "attention" to weigh the importance of different parts of the input sequence.

The field of neural networks is constantly evolving, with new architectures, training techniques, and applications being developed all the time. Researchers are exploring ways to make networks more efficient, more interpretable, and more robust. They are also investigating new paradigms like neuromorphic computing, which aims to build hardware that more closely mimics the structure and function of the biological brain.

So, from simple beginnings inspired by our understanding of the brain, neural networks have evolved into incredibly powerful tools that are driving much of the progress in modern AI. They learn by adjusting the connections between artificial neurons based on data, and the development of deeper architectures and specialized designs has enabled them to tackle increasingly complex and real-world problems. While still a simplification of the biological brain, they have proven to be remarkably effective at learning intricate patterns and making intelligent decisions.

Data: The Fuel of AI

Alright, let's talk about something absolutely fundamental to making AI work, something that's often called the "fuel" that powers the whole engine: data. You can have the most brilliant algorithms and the most powerful computers, but without the right kind of data, it's like having a fancy sports car with an empty gas tank – it's just not going anywhere.

Think about how we humans learn. We gather information from the world around us through our senses, we experience things, we read books, we listen to people talk. All of this sensory input and information forms the basis of our understanding and our ability to learn and make decisions. For AI, data plays a very similar role. It's the raw material from which AI systems learn patterns, make predictions, and ultimately exhibit what we call "intelligence."

Now, when we talk about data in the context of AI, we're not just talking about any old information. The kind of data that's useful for training AI systems often needs to have certain characteristics. For supervised learning, as we discussed, the data needs to be labeled. That means for each piece of input data (like an image or a text document), we also need to have the correct output or category associated with it (like "cat" or "not spam"). This labeled data is what allows the AI to learn the relationship between the inputs and the desired outputs.

Imagine trying to teach a child the difference between apples and oranges. You wouldn't just show them a bunch of fruits; you would also tell them, "This is an apple," and "This is an orange." The labels are crucial for the child to learn the distinguishing features. It's the same for AI. The labels provide the "ground truth" that the algorithm learns to match.

For unsupervised learning, the situation is a bit different. Here, we're feeding the AI unlabeled data and asking it to find patterns or structures on its own. It's like giving that child a pile of different fruits and saying, "See if you can find any groups or similarities among these." The AI has to figure out the underlying relationships in the data without any explicit guidance on what those relationships might be.

Then, for reinforcement learning, the data comes in the form of the agent's interactions with its environment and the rewards or penalties it receives for its actions. It's like the child learning to ride a bike through trial and error, feeling the wobble, falling, and eventually figuring out how to balance. The "data" here is the sequence of actions taken and the resulting feedback from the environment.

The amount of data is often a critical factor in the performance of AI systems, especially for complex tasks like image recognition or natural language processing. Deep learning models, in particular, tend to thrive on massive datasets. The more examples they see, the better they can learn the underlying patterns and the more accurate their predictions or decisions are likely to be. Think about learning to recognize different accents in a language – the more people you hear speaking with those accents, the better you become at distinguishing them.

But it's not just about quantity; the quality of the data is equally important, if not more so. If the data used to train an AI system is biased, inaccurate, or incomplete, the AI will likely reflect those flaws in its behavior. For example, if an image recognition system is primarily trained on pictures of cats with a certain breed or in a certain setting, it might not perform well on pictures of cats of different breeds or in different environments. Similarly, if a language model is trained on text that contains certain biases, it might perpetuate those biases in its own output.

A significant part of the AI development process involves data preparation and cleaning. This can include tasks like removing errors, handling missing values, normalizing data to a consistent scale, and transforming data into a format that the AI algorithm can understand. It's like a chef carefully selecting and preparing their ingredients before they start cooking to ensure the best possible outcome.

The relevance of the data to the task at hand is paramount. If you want to train an AI to translate English to Spanish, feeding it a dataset of medical images won't be very helpful. The data needs to be directly related to the problem you're trying to solve.

The way we collect, store, and manage this vast amounts of data is also a significant technological challenge. We need efficient databases, data pipelines, and infrastructure to handle the scale and complexity of the data used in modern AI. Cloud computing platforms have been instrumental in providing the necessary resources for this.

Data is the lifeblood of AI. It's the foundation upon which AI systems learn and improve. Without a steady supply of high-quality, relevant data, even the most sophisticated AI algorithms will be limited in their capabilities. As AI continues to evolve and tackle more complex problems, the importance of data will only continue to grow, making data management, quality control, and ethical considerations around data usage increasingly critical. It's a symbiotic relationship – AI needs data to learn, and the insights we gain from AI can often help us better understand and utilize our data.

Chapter 4: Key Disciplines and Methods in AI

So, let's really dig into the heart of how modern AI achieves its smarts, and that takes us straight to the concept of Machine Learning. You've heard the term, I'm sure, and it's often used interchangeably with AI, but it's more accurate to think of machine learning as a core *approach* or a set of techniques *within* the broader field of AI. It's essentially about teaching computers to learn from data without being explicitly programmed for every single task. Think of it as moving away from giving a computer a step-by-step instruction manual for everything and instead letting it learn the rules of the game by playing it over and over.

Now, the traditional way of programming a computer involves writing specific code that tells the computer exactly what to do in every situation. If the situation changes even slightly, the program might not know how to handle it. Machine learning offers a different paradigm. Instead of writing explicit rules, we feed the computer a whole bunch of data relevant to the task we want it to perform, and the machine learning algorithm figures out the underlying patterns and relationships in that data on its own. It learns from examples.

Think back to our example of teaching a child to recognize cats and dogs. We don't give the child a precise list of rules like "if it has pointy ears and a long tail, it's a cat; if it barks, it's a dog" because there are always exceptions and variations. Instead, we show the child many examples of cats and dogs, and the child gradually learns to identify the distinguishing features through experience. Machine learning algorithms work in a somewhat analogous way.

There are different "flavors" or types of machine learning, as we've already touched upon with supervised, unsupervised, and reinforcement learning. Each of these approaches has its own way of learning from data and is suited for different kinds of problems.

With supervised learning, remember, we have a "teacher" in the form of labeled data. The algorithm learns a mapping from inputs to outputs based on these examples. It's like learning with a textbook that has both the questions and the answers. The goal is to train a model that can accurately predict the output for new, unseen inputs. This is incredibly useful for tasks like classification (categorizing things, like identifying if an email is spam or not) and regression (predicting continuous values, like forecasting sales).

Then there's unsupervised learning, where the algorithm is left to its own devices with unlabeled data. It's like being given a huge collection of information and being asked to find any interesting patterns or groupings within it. Unsupervised learning is great for tasks like clustering (grouping similar data points together, like segmenting customers based on their purchasing behavior) and dimensionality reduction (simplifying complex data while retaining its essential structure).

And finally, reinforcement learning is all about learning through interaction and feedback. The algorithm, acting as an "agent," explores an environment and learns to take actions that maximize a reward signal. It's like learning to play a video game by trying different strategies and getting points for success and penalties for failure. This is powerful for tasks where there isn't a single "right" answer but a sequence of actions that leads to a goal, like training robots or developing game-playing AI.

Regardless of the specific type, the core idea behind machine learning is this: algorithms that can learn from data. These algorithms are designed to identify patterns, make inferences, and improve their performance over time as they are exposed to more data. They essentially build a model based on the training data, and this model is then used to make predictions or decisions on new data.

The process of building a machine learning model typically involves several steps. First, you need to collect and prepare your data. As we discussed, the quality and relevance of the data are crucial. Then, you choose an appropriate machine learning algorithm based on the type of problem you're trying to solve and the nature of your data. Next, you train the model by feeding it the training data and allowing the algorithm to learn the underlying patterns. After training, you need to evaluate the model's performance on a separate set of data that it hasn't seen before to see how well it generalizes. Finally, if the performance is satisfactory, you can deploy the model to make predictions or decisions in the real world.

Machine learning has been the driving force behind many of the recent advancements in AI. It's what allows our smartphones to recognize our faces, our online shopping sites to recommend products we might like, and our virtual assistants to (sometimes!) understand our commands. It's a powerful and versatile approach that is constantly evolving, with new algorithms and techniques being developed all the time. It's about giving computers the ability to learn and adapt, making them much more flexible and intelligent in the face of complex and ever-changing real-world scenarios.

Machine Learning Techniques

Okay, so we've established that machine learning is all about teaching computers to learn from data. But just like there are many different subjects you can study in school, there's a whole range of techniques and algorithms within machine learning that are used for different kinds of tasks and data. Let's take a stroll through some of the major players in this fascinating toolkit.

Starting with Supervised Learning, as we know, this is where we have labeled data, a clear "right answer" for each input. Within this broad category, there are several important techniques.

First, let's talk about Linear Regression. Imagine you're trying to predict the price of a house based on its size. If you have historical data of house sizes and their corresponding prices, you can use linear regression to find a line that best fits this data. This line then allows you to predict the price of a new house based on its size.

It's all about finding that straight-line relationship between variables.

Now, what if you want to predict something that has a limited number of outcomes, like whether an email is spam or not spam? That's where Logistic Regression comes in. Despite its name, it's actually used for classification rather than predicting continuous values. It uses a special function to model the probability of a certain outcome (like the probability of an email being spam) based on the input features.

Moving on, we have Decision Trees. Think of these as a series of questions that lead you to a decision. For example, to classify a fruit, you might first ask, "Is it red?" If yes, then "Is it round?" If yes again, then "Is it sweet?" and so on, until you reach a classification like "apple." Decision trees work in a similar way, creating a tree-like structure of rules based on the features in the data to make predictions.

Random Forests are like a whole bunch of decision trees working together. Instead of relying on a single tree, a random forest builds multiple decision trees on different subsets of the data and then combines their predictions to get a more robust and accurate result. It's like getting opinions from a whole panel of experts instead of just one.

Another powerful supervised learning technique is Support Vector Machines (SVMs). Imagine you have two groups of data points, say, representing cats and dogs on a graph. SVMs try to find the best line (or hyperplane in higher dimensions) that separates these two groups with the largest possible margin. This helps to create a robust classifier that can accurately categorize new data points.

And of course, we can't forget Neural Networks, especially the deep learning architectures we discussed. These are incredibly flexible and powerful models that can learn complex relationships in data through multiple layers of interconnected nodes. They've achieved state-of-the-art results in many areas, from image and speech recognition to natural language processing.

Now, let's switch gears and talk about Unsupervised Learning, where we don't have labeled data. One of the most common tasks here is Clustering. Algorithms like K-Means try to group data points into a predefined number of clusters based on their similarity. Imagine you have a scatter plot of customer data, and K-Means might identify natural groups of customers with similar purchasing habits.

Another important unsupervised learning technique is Dimensionality Reduction. Algorithms like Principal Component Analysis (PCA) aim to reduce the number of variables in a dataset while retaining as much of the important information as possible. This can be useful for visualizing high-dimensional data or for making it easier for other machine learning algorithms to process.

Association Rule Mining is another interesting unsupervised technique. Algorithms like Apriori try to find interesting relationships or associations between different items in a dataset. A classic example is market basket analysis, where you might discover that people who buy bread and milk also tend to buy eggs.

Let's touch on Reinforcement Learning. Here, the focus is on an agent learning to make decisions in an environment to maximize a reward. Some key techniques in reinforcement learning involve defining the agent, the environment, the possible actions the agent can take, the states of the environment, and the reward function that guides the learning process. Algorithms like Q-learning and Deep Q-Networks (DQNs) are used to learn optimal policies (strategies for choosing actions) through trial and error.

It's important to understand that this is just a glimpse into the vast landscape of machine learning techniques. There are many more algorithms and variations within these categories, and the field is constantly evolving with new approaches being developed. The choice of which technique to use depends heavily on the specific problem you're trying to solve, the type and amount of data you have, and the desired outcome. It's like a chef having a wide array of knives, each best suited for a particular cutting task. Understanding these different tools is key to effectively applying machine learning to real-world problems.

Applications for Machine Learning

Okay, so we've talked about the nuts and bolts of machine learning – how it works, the different types of learning, and some of the common techniques. Now, let's take a look at where all this cleverness is actually being used in the real world, across various industries that you might encounter every day. It's pretty amazing how machine learning is quietly revolutionizing so many aspects of how businesses operate and how we live our lives.

Think about e-commerce and retail. Machine learning is a total game-changer here. Remember those product recommendations you see when you're browsing online? That's often machine learning at work, analyzing your past purchases, browsing history, and even what other people with similar tastes have bought to suggest things you might like. It's like having a super-personalized shopping assistant. Beyond recommendations, machine learning is also used for things like fraud detection in online transactions, optimizing pricing strategies based on demand and competitor prices, managing inventory to predict what products will be popular and when, and even personalizing the entire shopping experience, from the layout of the website to the marketing emails you receive. It's all about understanding customer behavior and tailoring the experience to individual needs.

Then there's the healthcare industry, which is seeing a huge impact from machine learning. Imagine AI systems that can analyze medical images like X-rays or MRIs to help doctors detect diseases like cancer earlier and with greater accuracy. That's becoming a reality thanks to machine learning. It's also being used to predict which patients are at high risk of developing certain conditions, to personalize treatment plans based on a patient's genetic makeup and medical history, to discover new drugs by analyzing vast amounts of biological data, and even to automate some of the more administrative tasks, freeing up healthcare professionals to focus on patient care. It's about making healthcare more efficient, more personalized, and ultimately more effective.

The financial services industry is another big adopter of machine learning. We already mentioned fraud detection, but it goes way beyond that. Machine learning is used for credit risk assessment, helping banks decide who is likely to repay a loan. It's used in algorithmic trading to make split-second decisions in the stock market. It's helping financial institutions understand their customers better, offer personalized financial advice, and even automate customer service through intelligent chatbots. It's all about managing risk, improving efficiency, and providing better customer experiences in a highly regulated and data-rich environment.

Manufacturing is also being transformed by machine learning. Think about predictive maintenance – using sensors on machinery to collect data and then using machine learning to predict when a piece of equipment is likely to fail. This allows companies to schedule maintenance proactively, reducing downtime and saving money. Machine learning is also used for quality control, analyzing images of products on the assembly line to identify defects, and for optimizing production processes to improve efficiency and reduce waste. It's about making factories smarter and more efficient.

Even the way we travel is being impacted. Self-driving cars, while still under development, rely heavily on machine learning to perceive their surroundings, make decisions, and navigate roads safely. Machine learning is also used in route optimization for delivery services, predicting traffic patterns to improve travel times, and personalizing the in-car experience. It's about making transportation safer, more efficient, and more convenient.

The energy sector is also leveraging machine learning. It can be used to predict energy demand, optimize the operation of power grids, detect anomalies in equipment to prevent failures, and even help in the discovery of new energy sources. It's about making the energy system more reliable, efficient, and sustainable.

And let's not forget the media and entertainment industry. We already talked about recommendation systems for movies and music, but machine learning is also used for things like content generation (think about AI writing articles or creating music), analyzing audience engagement to understand what types of content are most popular, and even detecting fake news and harmful content online. It's about personalizing experiences and managing the flow of information.

These are just some of the many industries where machine learning is making a significant impact. From agriculture to education, from security to marketing, machine learning is being applied to solve complex problems, automate tasks, improve efficiency, personalize experiences, and drive innovation. As the technology continues to advance and we generate more and more data, we can only expect the applications of machine learning to become even more widespread and transformative in the years to come. It's a truly versatile tool that's helping to shape the future of how we live and work.

Deep Learning

Okay, let's really zoom in on a particularly hot and powerful area within machine learning: Deep Learning. You hear this term a lot these days, and it's responsible for many of the really impressive AI feats you've probably encountered, like incredibly accurate image recognition, remarkably fluent language translation, and even AI that can generate realistic-sounding speech. At its heart, deep learning is a type of machine learning that uses artificial neural networks with multiple layers to progressively extract higher-level features from the raw input data. Think of it like building a very complex and sophisticated processing system inspired, in a very loose way, by how our own brains work.

Remember those artificial neurons and neural networks we talked about before? Well, deep learning takes that basic idea and stacks many, many of these layers together – sometimes dozens, even hundreds. The "deep" in deep learning simply refers to the depth of these neural networks, the number of layers they contain. This increased depth allows the network to learn incredibly intricate and hierarchical representations of data.

Imagine you're trying to teach a computer to recognize a cat in a picture using a traditional, "shallow" neural network with just a few layers. The first layer might learn to detect basic features like edges and corners in the image. The next layer might combine these edges and corners to recognize simple shapes like circles or lines. Finally, the output layer might try to combine these shapes to say, "Okay, this looks like a cat."

Now, with deep learning, we have many more layers in between. The first few layers might still learn those basic edges and corners. But then, as the information flows through the deeper layers, the network can learn to recognize increasingly complex features – maybe textures like fur, parts of the face like eyes and ears, and then combinations of these parts that eventually form the whole concept of a cat. Each layer builds upon the features learned in the previous layer, creating a hierarchy of abstraction.

This ability to automatically learn these hierarchical features directly from the raw data is one of the key strengths of deep learning. In older machine learning approaches, engineers often had to manually design and extract relevant features from the data before feeding it into the algorithm. This "feature engineering" could be a time-consuming and expertise-dependent process. Deep learning largely automates this, allowing the network to learn the most useful features for the task at hand.

Think about processing images again. Instead of manually trying to define what makes a cat a cat (e.g., pointy ears, whiskers), you just feed a deep learning network a massive dataset of cat and non-cat images, and the network learns to identify those distinguishing features on its own, often in ways that humans might not even explicitly think about.

Deep learning has been particularly successful in areas where the raw data is very complex and high-dimensional, like images, audio, and text. These types of data have intricate structures and patterns that can be effectively captured by deep, multi-layered networks.

For example, in computer vision, deep learning models called Convolutional Neural Networks (CNNs) have revolutionized tasks like image classification, object detection (identifying and locating objects within an image), and image segmentation (dividing an image into regions corresponding to different objects or parts). The convolutional layers in CNNs are particularly good at detecting spatial hierarchies of features in images.

In natural language processing (NLP), deep learning models like Recurrent Neural Networks (RNNs) and, more recently, Transformer networks have led to huge advancements in tasks like machine translation, text generation, sentiment analysis (determining the emotional tone of text), and question answering. These architectures are designed to handle sequential data like text, where the order of words is crucial for understanding meaning. Transformer networks, with their attention mechanisms, have been particularly groundbreaking in understanding the relationships between different parts of a sentence or even across long passages of text.

In speech recognition, deep learning models can now transcribe spoken language into text with remarkable accuracy, even in noisy environments. They learn to map the complex acoustic signals to the corresponding phonetic units and words.

The training of these deep networks requires a lot of data and significant computational power, as we've discussed before. The sheer number of connections and parameters in these deep models means they need to see a vast number of examples to learn effectively and avoid overfitting (memorizing the training data instead of generalizing to new data). The availability of large datasets and the advancements in hardware like GPUs have been crucial in enabling the deep learning revolution.

While incredibly powerful, deep learning isn't a magic bullet for all AI problems. It often requires a lot of data, can be computationally expensive to train, and the learned representations can sometimes be difficult to interpret (it can be hard to understand exactly why a deep learning model made a particular decision). It's also an active area of research to make deep learning models more robust, more data-efficient, and more explainable.

Deep learning has undeniably transformed the field of AI and continues to drive many of the exciting advancements we see today. Its ability to automatically learn complex features from raw data has unlocked new possibilities in a wide range of applications, bringing us closer to creating truly intelligent machines.

Understanding Neural Networks

Now, let's really get under the hood of these neural networks and explore some of the ways they're structured, especially when we talk about "deep learning architectures." Think of a basic neural network like a simple circuit with inputs, some processing in the middle, and an output. Deep learning architectures are like incredibly complex and intricate versions of these circuits, designed in specific ways to tackle different kinds of problems.

We already know that the fundamental building block is the artificial neuron, which takes inputs, applies weights and a bias, and then passes the result through an activation function. When you connect many of these neurons together in layers, you get a basic feedforward neural network. The information flows in one direction – from the input layer, through one or more hidden layers, to the output layer. These are the workhorses for many tasks, especially where the input has a fixed size, like a picture of a certain dimension or a set of measurements.

But the world isn't always so neatly structured. Sometimes we deal with sequences of data, like text where the order of words matters, or time series data where the order of events is crucial. For these kinds of problems, we often turn to Recurrent Neural Networks (RNNs). The key innovation in RNNs is that they have connections that loop back on themselves, allowing them to maintain a kind of "memory" of past inputs. Imagine reading a sentence – your understanding of a word often depends on the words that came before it. RNNs try to capture this idea by feeding the output of a neuron at one time step back into the network as an input at the next time step. This allows them to process sequences and learn dependencies over time.

However, basic RNNs can struggle with very long sequences. The "memory" can fade over longer distances, making it difficult to learn long-range dependencies. To address this, more sophisticated RNN architectures have been developed, most notably Long Short-Term Memory (LSTM) networks and Gated Recurrent Units (GRUs). These architectures introduce special "gates" that can control the flow of information within the network, allowing them to selectively remember important information over longer sequences and forget irrelevant details. Think of these gates as being able to decide when to store a piece of information in the network's "long-term memory" and when to discard it. LSTMs and GRUs have been incredibly successful in tasks like language modeling (predicting the next word in a sentence), machine translation, and speech recognition.

Now, let's shift our focus to a type of architecture that has revolutionized image and video processing: Convolutional Neural Networks (CNNs). When you look at an image, the spatial relationships between pixels are really important. A CNN is designed to exploit this spatial structure. Its main building block is the convolutional layer, which doesn't just connect every input neuron to every output neuron in the next layer (like in a basic feedforward network). Instead, it uses small "filters" that slide over the input image, performing a convolution operation. This operation essentially detects local patterns, like edges, corners, or textures, regardless of where they are located in the image.

Think of it like using a small magnifying glass to look at different parts of an image. Each filter acts like a specific pattern detector. By using many different filters, a CNN can learn to detect a wide range of features at different spatial locations. After convolutional layers, CNNs often include pooling layers, which reduce the spatial size of the representation, making the network more robust to small shifts and distortions in the input image. By stacking multiple convolutional and pooling layers, CNNs can learn to recognize increasingly complex and abstract features, eventually leading to a high-level understanding of the image content, like identifying objects or classifying the scene.

More recently, a different type of architecture has taken the natural language processing world by storm: Transformer networks. Unlike RNNs, which process sequences step by step, Transformers can process the entire input sequence in parallel. Their key innovation is the attention mechanism, which allows the network to weigh the importance of different parts of the input when processing a particular position. Imagine reading a long sentence and being able to instantly focus on the words that are most relevant to understanding the current word. The attention mechanism allows the Transformer to do something similar.

Transformer networks have proven to be incredibly powerful for a wide range of NLP tasks, including machine translation, text summarization, and question answering. They've also found applications in other domains like computer vision. Architectures like BERT (Bidirectional Encoder Representations from Transformers) and GPT (Generative Pre-trained Transformer) are based on the Transformer and have achieved remarkable results in understanding and generating human language.

Beyond these core architectures, there are many variations and combinations. For instance, you might see networks that combine convolutional layers for feature extraction from images with recurrent layers for processing sequences of images in a video. There's also a lot of research into things like graph neural networks for processing data that is structured as graphs (like social networks or molecules) and autoencoders which are used for unsupervised learning tasks like dimensionality reduction and anomaly detection.

The field of deep learning architecture design is constantly evolving. Researchers are always experimenting with new ways to connect neurons, new types of layers, and new training techniques to improve performance, efficiency, and interpretability. It's a very active and exciting area of research, constantly pushing the boundaries of what AI can do. Understanding these basic architectures gives you a glimpse into the diverse ways that neural networks can be structured to learn from different kinds of data and solve a wide array of complex problems.

Real-World Applications

Okay, so we've spent some time exploring the inner workings of deep learning, these intricate neural networks that can learn so much from data. Now, let's take a look at where all this sophistication is actually making a tangible difference in the world around us. You might be surprised at just how many aspects of modern life are already being touched, and in some cases, completely transformed by deep learning.

Think about your smartphone. When you use facial recognition to unlock it, that's often deep learning in action. These models have been trained on massive datasets of faces to learn the unique patterns that identify you, and they can do it with impressive speed and accuracy, even in different lighting conditions or if you're wearing glasses. It's a convenient and secure way to protect your personal information, all powered by deep neural networks.

And while you're on your phone, if you use a voice assistant to ask a question or give a command, you're interacting with another powerful application of deep learning. These systems use deep learning for speech recognition, transcribing your spoken words into text, and for natural language understanding, figuring out the meaning behind your request. The advancements in deep learning have made these assistants much more accurate and capable of handling a wider range of queries and commands, making them feel increasingly natural to interact with.

Now, let's move beyond your personal devices. Consider the healthcare industry. We touched on this with machine learning in general, but deep learning is taking it to a whole new level. Think about medical imaging analysis. Deep learning models can be trained to analyze X-rays, MRIs, and CT scans to detect subtle signs of disease, like tumors or anomalies, often with accuracy comparable to or even exceeding that of human experts. This can lead to earlier diagnosis and better treatment outcomes. In drug discovery, deep learning is being used to analyze vast amounts of biological and chemical data to identify potential drug candidates and predict their effectiveness, significantly speeding up the process of bringing new medicines to market. There's also work being done on using deep learning to personalize treatments based on a patient's individual genetic makeup and medical history.

The automotive industry is another area where deep learning is driving major innovation, most notably in the development of self-driving cars. These autonomous vehicles rely heavily on deep learning to process the massive amounts of data coming from their sensors (cameras, lidar, radar) in real-time. Deep learning models are used for tasks like object detection (identifying pedestrians, other vehicles, traffic signs), lane keeping, and predicting the behavior of other road users. While fully autonomous driving is still a work in progress, deep learning is the key technology making it a realistic possibility.

Think about how you consume media and entertainment. The recommendation systems on streaming platforms like Netflix or Spotify are often powered by deep learning. These systems analyze your viewing or listening history, as well as the behavior of other users with similar tastes, to suggest content you might enjoy. Deep learning models can learn very complex patterns in user preferences, leading to surprisingly accurate and personalized recommendations. Beyond recommendations, deep learning is also being used for content creation, with AI models now capable of generating realistic-sounding music, writing articles, and even creating art.

The financial services industry relies heavily on deep learning for a variety of critical tasks. Fraud detection is a big one, with deep learning models able to analyze vast amounts of transaction data to identify patterns that might indicate fraudulent activity, often in real-time. In algorithmic trading, deep learning can be used to analyze market trends and make high-speed trading decisions. It's also being applied to credit risk assessment, helping lenders to better predict the likelihood of borrowers defaulting on loans.

Even in manufacturing and logistics, deep learning is making a significant impact. For quality control, deep learning models can be trained to analyze images of products on the assembly line to identify even subtle defects that might be missed by human inspectors, leading to improved product quality and reduced waste. In supply chain optimization, deep learning can be used to predict demand, optimize inventory levels, and improve the efficiency of delivery routes.

And let's not forget the role of deep learning in natural language processing. We've already mentioned voice assistants and machine translation, but deep learning is also powering advancements in sentiment analysis (understanding the emotional tone of text, which is valuable for customer feedback analysis), text summarization (automatically generating concise summaries of long documents), and even chatbot technology, making virtual assistants more conversational and helpful.

These are just a few examples of the many real-world applications of deep learning. It's a technology that is rapidly evolving and finding its way into more and more aspects of our lives and industries. From making our personal devices smarter to revolutionizing healthcare and transportation, deep learning is proving to be a powerful tool for tackling complex problems and creating new possibilities. As we continue to generate more data and develop more sophisticated deep learning models, we can only expect its impact on the world to grow even further.

Natural Language Processing

Next, let's dive into a fascinating area of Artificial Intelligence that deals specifically with how computers can understand, interpret, and even generate human language. This field is called Natural Language Processing, or NLP for short. Think about all the ways we humans use language – we speak, we write, we read, we listen. It's how we communicate, share ideas, and connect with each other. NLP is all about enabling computers to do some of these same things.

Now, you might think that dealing with language would be straightforward for computers, since they're so good with numbers and logic. But human language is incredibly complex and nuanced. It's full of ambiguities, different grammatical structures, slang, sarcasm, and context-dependent meanings. What we say isn't always exactly what we mean, and understanding that requires a lot more than just processing words on a page. That's where NLP comes in – it's the art and science of making computers linguistically savvy.

At its core, NLP involves a whole range of techniques and algorithms that allow computers to process and analyze text and speech. Think of it as giving a computer a set of tools to dissect language, understand its components, and then use that understanding to perform various tasks.

One of the fundamental tasks in NLP is parsing, which is like breaking down a sentence into its grammatical parts – identifying the nouns, verbs, adjectives, and how they all relate to each other. It's like diagramming sentences in school, but getting a computer to do it automatically is a pretty intricate process.

Another key area is text analysis, which involves extracting meaningful information from text. This can include things like sentiment analysis, where the goal is to determine the emotional tone expressed in a piece of text – whether it's positive, negative, or neutral. This is incredibly useful for businesses wanting to understand customer feedback from reviews or social media.

Topic modeling is another text analysis technique that aims to identify the main topics or themes discussed within a collection of documents. Imagine having thousands of news articles and wanting to automatically figure out what the major subjects being covered are. Topic modeling can help with that.

Then we have information extraction, which focuses on identifying and extracting specific pieces of information from text, like names of people, organizations, locations, dates, and relationships between them. This can be used to automatically populate databases or to summarize key facts from large amounts of text.

NLP also deals with language generation, which is the opposite of understanding – it's about getting computers to produce human-like text. This can range from simple tasks like generating automated responses in a chatbot to more complex tasks like writing articles or even creating creative content.

One of the big challenges in NLP is dealing with ambiguity. Human language is full of it. A single word can have multiple meanings depending on the context ("bank" can refer to a financial institution or the side of a river). A sentence can be interpreted in different ways based on how the words are grouped or the surrounding text. Getting a computer to correctly resolve these ambiguities is a crucial part of NLP.

Another challenge is understanding context. We humans rely heavily on the context of a conversation or a piece of writing to understand its meaning. Computers need to be able to do this as well, which often involves having some form of "memory" of what has been discussed before or knowledge about the real world.

Over the years, NLP has evolved significantly. Early approaches often relied on handcrafted rules and statistical methods. But with the rise of machine learning, and particularly deep learning, NLP has made huge leaps forward. Deep learning models, especially architectures like Recurrent Neural Networks (RNNs) and Transformers, have proven incredibly effective at learning complex patterns in language from large amounts of data.

Think about machine translation. Early translation systems were often clunky and produced awkward-sounding results. But with deep learning-based NLP, translation has become much more fluent and accurate, making it easier for people who speak different languages to communicate.

Chatbots have also become much more sophisticated thanks to NLP. Modern chatbots can understand a wider range of user queries, hold more natural-sounding conversations, and even provide personalized assistance.

Search engines rely heavily on NLP to understand what you're searching for, even if you use natural language queries, and to provide you with relevant results.

Sentiment analysis powered by deep learning is used extensively by businesses to understand customer opinions from social media, product reviews, and surveys, allowing them to gain valuable insights into their brand and products.

Content summarization tools can now automatically generate concise summaries of long articles or documents, saving us time and effort.

NLP is a vast and rapidly evolving field that sits at the intersection of computer science, linguistics, and artificial intelligence. Its goal is to bridge the gap between human communication and computer understanding, and as it continues to advance, it's likely to have an even greater impact on how we interact with technology and with each other. It's about making computers truly understand our world, expressed in the words we use every day.

How AI Interprets Language

Let's really get into the fascinating process of how AI manages to do something that seems so uniquely human: understanding and generating language. It's not as simple as just knowing a dictionary and some grammar rules; there's a whole lot more going on under the hood. Think of it like trying to teach someone a new language – you don't just give them a list of words; you need to teach them how those words fit together, the nuances of meaning, and even how to use them in different social situations. AI tackles language in a similarly layered way.

When we talk about AI understanding language, the first step often involves breaking down the raw text or speech into smaller, manageable units. For text, this might involve tokenization, which is essentially splitting the text into individual words or punctuation marks. For speech, it involves speech recognition, which is a whole complex process in itself, turning the audio signals into a sequence of words.

Once the language is in a digital form that the AI can process, the next challenge is to understand the meaning. This is where things get interesting. Early approaches to NLP often relied on handcrafted rules and statistical models. For example, to understand the grammatical structure of a sentence, a system might use a set of rules about how different parts of speech can be combined. To understand the meaning of a word, it might look it up in a digital dictionary.

These rule-based systems were often brittle and struggled with the inherent flexibility and ambiguity of human language. Modern AI, especially with the rise of machine learning and deep learning, takes a much more data-driven approach. Instead of explicitly programming all the rules, we feed the AI massive amounts of text and speech data and let it learn the patterns and relationships on its own.

One key technique in modern NLP for understanding language is word embeddings. Imagine taking every word in a language and representing it as a point in a high-dimensional space. The idea behind word embeddings is that words that are semantically similar (i.e., have similar meanings or are used in similar contexts) will be located closer to each other in this space. These embeddings are learned from large amounts of text data, allowing the AI to capture subtle relationships between words that a simple dictionary lookup wouldn't reveal. For example, the embeddings for "king" and "queen" would likely be closer to each other than the embeddings for "king" and "bicycle."

Building on word embeddings, deep learning models, particularly Recurrent Neural Networks (RNNs) and Transformer networks, play a crucial role in understanding the context of words within a sentence or a longer piece of text. RNNs, with their ability to maintain a kind of "memory" of previous words, can process sentences sequentially and understand how the meaning of a word can be influenced by the words around it. Transformer networks, with their attention mechanisms, can even better capture these contextual relationships by allowing the model to weigh the importance of different words in the input when processing a particular word.

For example, consider the sentence "The cat sat on the mat." To understand the role of each word and the overall meaning, the AI needs to know that "cat" is the subject, "sat" is the verb, and "mat" is the object, and how these relate to each other. Deep learning models trained on vast amounts of text can learn these grammatical structures and semantic relationships implicitly.

When it comes to AI generating language, the process is somewhat the reverse of understanding, but it's equally complex. The AI needs to decide what it wants to say, how to phrase it grammatically correctly, and how to choose the right words to convey the intended meaning.

Again, early language generation systems often relied on predefined templates and rules. For example, a chatbot might have a template like "Hello [user name], how can I help you today?" and it would just fill in the user's name. While simple, this approach lacked flexibility and could sound very robotic.

Modern AI language generation, especially with deep learning, is much more sophisticated. Models like language models are trained on massive amounts of text data to predict the next word in a sequence. By repeatedly predicting the next word, they can generate coherent and often surprisingly human-like text.

Think about how these models work. They take an input, which could be a prompt or the beginning of a sentence, and then they predict the most likely next word based on the patterns they learned from the training data. Then, that predicted word becomes part of the input for predicting the next word, and so on. By carefully controlling this process, we can get the AI to generate paragraphs, articles, or even creative writing.

The quality of the generated text depends heavily on the size and diversity of the training data and the complexity of the language model. Models like GPT (Generative Pre-trained Transformer) have shown impressive abilities in generating text that is often difficult to distinguish from human-written content.

Even with these advancements, AI understanding and generation of language is not perfect. AI can still struggle with truly understanding the nuances of human conversation, including sarcasm, humor, and implicit meanings. Generated text can sometimes lack coherence over longer passages or can reflect biases present in the training data.

The progress in NLP has been remarkable. AI is now capable of understanding and generating language in ways that were once considered science fiction. From virtual assistants that can answer our questions to translation tools that break down language barriers, and from chatbots that provide customer service to AI that can help us write creative content, the applications of AI in understanding and generating language are becoming increasingly integrated into our daily lives. It's a testament to the power of data-driven learning and the ingenuity of the algorithms that are making computers more linguistically intelligent.

Practical NLP

Okay, so we've talked about the fascinating science behind how AI can understand and generate language. Now, let's bring it down to earth and look at some of the really practical ways this technology, often grouped under the umbrella of Natural Language Processing (NLP), is being used in applications you might encounter, or even use, every single day. Think of it as seeing the blueprints of a fantastic machine and then seeing that machine actually in action, performing useful tasks.

One of the most visible and talked-about applications of NLP is in chatbots. You've probably interacted with one at some point, maybe when you had a question on a company's website or through a customer service app. Early chatbots were often quite basic, relying on predefined scripts and keyword matching. If you didn't use the exact right words, they'd get confused. But modern chatbots, powered by sophisticated NLP techniques, are a whole different ballgame.

These advanced chatbots can understand a much wider range of natural language, parse your questions, and even understand the intent behind them. They use techniques like sentiment analysis to gauge your emotional state and tailor their responses accordingly. They can access and process information from vast databases to answer your queries, guide you through processes, and even troubleshoot problems. Think about a chatbot that can not only answer "What's your return policy?" but also understand follow-up questions like "What if I don't have the original receipt?" and provide relevant information. These intelligent virtual assistants are becoming increasingly integrated into customer service, providing 24/7 support and handling a large volume of inquiries, freeing up human agents to deal with more complex issues.

Another incredibly practical application of NLP is in machine translation tools. Remember the days when translating a document meant painstakingly going through it word by word with a dictionary? Now, with just a few clicks, we can get reasonably accurate translations between a multitude of languages, thanks to NLP. These tools, especially those powered by deep learning, don't just translate word for word; they understand the context of the sentence and try to preserve the meaning and even the nuances of the original text.

Think about how invaluable this is in our increasingly globalized world. It allows people from different linguistic backgrounds to communicate more easily, access information in different languages, and conduct international business more smoothly. While machine translation isn't perfect yet – it can still sometimes miss subtle cultural references or idioms – it has come a long way and is an indispensable tool for millions of people.

Beyond direct communication, NLP is also heavily used in information retrieval, which is essentially what powers search engines. When you type a query into a search bar, NLP techniques are used to understand the meaning behind your words, identify relevant keywords, and match them with the vast amount of information available online. Search engines use NLP to understand synonyms, related terms, and the intent behind your search to provide you with the most relevant results, even if the exact words you used don't appear on the page.

NLP also plays a crucial role in text analysis for business intelligence. Companies are sitting on mountains of textual data – customer reviews, social media posts, survey responses, support tickets, news articles. NLP tools can analyze this unstructured data at scale, extracting valuable insights into customer sentiment, emerging trends, product feedback, and brand perception. This information can then be used to make better business decisions, improve products and services, and understand their customers on a deeper level.

Think about a company launching a new product. By using NLP to analyze social media chatter and customer reviews, they can quickly get a sense of how the product is being received, identify any common issues or praises, and respond accordingly. This real-time feedback loop is incredibly valuable.

Another practical application is in content moderation. With the explosion of online content, it's a huge challenge to monitor and filter out harmful or inappropriate material. NLP techniques are being used to automatically identify and flag hate speech, abusive language, misinformation, and other types of undesirable content, helping to create safer and more positive online environments.

NLP is also finding its way into content creation. While we're not quite at the point of AI writing the next great novel, NLP tools can assist with tasks like generating summaries of long documents, creating product descriptions, and even drafting initial versions of articles or reports. These tools can help to improve efficiency and free up human writers to focus on more creative and strategic aspects of content creation.

In the realm of education, NLP is being used to develop intelligent tutoring systems that can understand student questions in natural language, provide personalized feedback, and even adapt their teaching methods based on the student's learning style. It can also be used to automatically grade essays and provide constructive criticism.

Think about accessibility. NLP-powered tools like screen readers and voice recognition software are crucial for individuals with disabilities, allowing them to interact with technology and access information in ways that would otherwise be impossible.

From the seemingly simple interactions with chatbots to the complex analysis of global information, NLP is a workhorse technology that underpins many of the intelligent systems we rely on today. It's a testament to the power of teaching machines to understand and use the most fundamental tool of human connection: language. And as NLP continues to advance, we can expect to see even more innovative and practical applications emerge in the years to come, making our interactions with technology feel increasingly natural and intuitive.

Computer Vision

Now let's talk about something truly fascinating: how we can teach computers to "see" and interpret the world around them, much like we humans do with our eyes and brains. This field is called Computer Vision, and it's a crucial part of Artificial Intelligence that's enabling all sorts of amazing applications, from self-driving cars to medical image analysis. Think about it – our vision is so fundamental to how we navigate and understand the world. Giving that capability to machines opens up a universe of possibilities.

When we look at an image, whether it's a photograph or a video frame, it's essentially just a grid of pixels, each with its own color and intensity information. For a computer, it's just a big array of numbers. The challenge of computer vision is to take this raw numerical data and extract meaningful information from it – to identify objects, understand scenes, track movement, and ultimately, to make sense of the visual world.

Early approaches to computer vision often involved trying to program computers with explicit rules about what different objects look like. For example, you might try to define a "car" by its rectangular shape, wheels, and windows. But as you can imagine, this approach is incredibly brittle. Cars come in all shapes and sizes, viewed from different angles, in different lighting conditions, and often partially occluded. Trying to write enough rules to cover all these variations is a monumental and ultimately impractical task.

This is where machine learning, and especially deep learning, has revolutionized the field of computer vision. Instead of trying to hand-code rules, we feed computers massive amounts of visual data – millions of images and videos – and let them learn the patterns and features that are characteristic of different objects and scenes.

Think back to how we teach a child to recognize a cat. We don't give them a list of precise rules; we just show them lots of pictures of cats (and non-cats) and say "cat." The child's brain learns to identify the visual features that are consistently associated with cats. Deep learning models, particularly Convolutional Neural Networks (CNNs), work in a somewhat similar way.

As we discussed before, CNNs use layers of artificial neurons that are specifically designed to process grid-like data like images. These layers contain convolutional filters that slide over the image, learning to detect local patterns like edges, corners, textures, and simple shapes. By stacking multiple convolutional layers, the network can learn to recognize increasingly complex and abstract features, eventually combining these features to identify whole objects or understand entire scenes.

For example, in an image recognition task, the early layers of a CNN might learn to detect edges and simple curves. The middle layers might combine these to recognize parts of objects, like a wheel or a cat's ear. The later layers would then combine these parts to recognize the entire object, like a car or a cat.

One of the key challenges in computer vision is object recognition – identifying what objects are present in an image and sometimes even where they are located. Deep learning models have become incredibly good at this, achieving near-human-level performance on some tasks. This is what powers things like the object recognition in your smartphone's camera or the ability of self-driving cars to "see" pedestrians and other vehicles.

Beyond just identifying objects, computer vision also deals with object detection, which involves not only recognizing the objects but also drawing bounding boxes around them to indicate their location in the image. This is crucial for applications like autonomous driving or robotic navigation.

Image segmentation is another related task, where the goal is to assign a label to each pixel in an image, effectively dividing the image into regions corresponding to different objects or parts of objects. This provides a much more detailed understanding of the scene than just object detection.

Computer vision also encompasses video analysis, which adds the dimension of time. This involves tasks like object tracking (following an object as it moves through a video), action recognition (identifying what actions are taking place in a video), and even understanding the overall activity or scene depicted in a video. This is essential for applications like surveillance, sports analysis, and understanding human behavior.

Another important area is image generation, where AI models are trained to create new images from textual descriptions or other input. This has led to some fascinating and sometimes surprising results, with AI now capable of generating photorealistic images of objects, scenes, and even people that don't exist.

Computer vision is also being used in a wide range of specialized applications. In medical imaging, as we touched on, it can help doctors analyze scans and detect diseases. In agriculture, it can be used to monitor crop health, detect pests, and optimize irrigation. In manufacturing, it can be used for quality control and robotic guidance. In security, it powers facial recognition systems and helps with surveillance.

The field of computer vision is constantly advancing, driven by new research in deep learning architectures, the availability of larger and more diverse datasets, and the increasing computational power of our hardware. As AI continues to evolve, our ability to teach computers to see and understand the visual world will only become more sophisticated, leading to even more transformative applications in the future. It's about giving machines a fundamental sense that we humans rely on every single moment, and the possibilities are truly limitless.

AI Image Recognition

Let's zoom in on a really captivating area where Artificial Intelligence shows some of its most impressive abilities: image recognition. Think about how effortlessly you can glance at a picture and instantly identify what's in it – a cat, a car, a friend's face. It seems so simple, something we take for granted. But teaching a computer to do the same thing, and to do it reliably and accurately, is a complex and fascinating challenge that AI has made tremendous strides in tackling.

At its core, image recognition is about enabling computers to "see" and understand the content of digital images. This might involve identifying what objects are present, where they are located within the image, and sometimes even understanding the context or the relationship between different elements in the scene.

Now, as we touched on when we talked about computer vision in general, the initial approaches to image recognition were quite rudimentary. They often involved trying to define objects based on simple features like their shape, size, or color. Imagine trying to tell a computer that a cat is a small, furry thing with pointy ears and a tail. While this might work for some cats in ideal conditions, it would quickly fall apart when faced with cats of different breeds, in different poses, or partially hidden behind other objects. The real world is just too messy and variable for such simplistic rules to work reliably.

The breakthrough in image recognition came with the rise of machine learning, and particularly deep learning, specifically using Convolutional Neural Networks (CNNs). These architectures, as we discussed, are inspired by how the visual cortex in our own brains processes information. They are designed to automatically learn hierarchical features from raw pixel data.

Think about how a CNN might learn to recognize a dog. You feed it a massive dataset of images, many of which are labeled as "dog" and many as "not dog." The network starts by looking for very basic patterns in the pixels, like edges and corners. As the information flows through deeper layers of the network, these basic features are combined to detect more complex patterns, like textures (fur), shapes (circles for eyes, triangles for ears), and then even combinations of these shapes that start to resemble parts of a dog. Finally, the very last layers of the network learn to recognize the overall arrangement of these high-level features that uniquely identify a dog.

The beauty of this approach is that the network learns these features automatically from the data. We don't have to manually tell it what to look for. The network figures out the most relevant visual cues that distinguish a dog from a cat, a car, or any other object in its training data.

This ability to learn complex, hierarchical representations is what makes deep learning so powerful for image recognition. By having many layers, the network can build up increasingly abstract and meaningful features, going from simple edges to whole objects.

One of the key tasks within image recognition is image classification, where the goal is to assign a label to an entire image, indicating what it contains (e.g., "this is a picture of a cat"). Another related task is object detection, which goes a step further by not only identifying the objects present but also drawing bounding boxes around them to show their location within the image (e.g., "there is a cat at these coordinates").

Then there's image segmentation, where the goal is to assign a label to each individual pixel in the image, effectively outlining the boundaries of different objects and regions. This provides a much more detailed understanding of the scene than just knowing what objects are present.

The applications of AI in image recognition are already widespread and continue to grow. Think about social media, where AI is used to automatically identify faces in photos, allowing you to tag your friends. It's also used to filter content, for example, by identifying and removing inappropriate images.

In the security industry, facial recognition technology powered by deep learning is used for access control and surveillance. It can be used to verify identities and detect suspicious activity.

Medical imaging analysis is another area where AI-powered image recognition is making a huge difference. Deep learning models can be trained to analyze medical scans like X-rays, MRIs, and CT scans to detect signs of disease, often with remarkable accuracy, assisting doctors in making faster and more reliable diagnoses.

Autonomous vehicles rely heavily on image recognition to understand their surroundings. They need to be able to identify pedestrians, other vehicles, traffic signs, and obstacles in real-time to navigate safely. Deep learning models are crucial for this task, processing the data from cameras and other sensors to build a comprehensive understanding of the driving environment.

In retail, image recognition is used for things like product identification (think about scanning a barcode with your phone), visual search (allowing you to search for products based on an image), and even analyzing customer behavior in stores.

In agriculture, AI-powered image recognition can be used to monitor crop health, detect diseases or pests, and even guide automated harvesting equipment.

The field is constantly evolving, with researchers developing new and more efficient network architectures and training techniques to improve accuracy, speed, and robustness. As we gather more data and refine our models, the capabilities of AI in image recognition will only continue to advance, leading to even more innovative and impactful applications in the future. It's about giving machines a powerful sense of sight and the ability to interpret the visual world around us, opening up a whole new realm of possibilities for automation, analysis, and understanding.

Current Applications

Okay, let's take a good look around at where Artificial Intelligence is actually popping up in the world right now, in ways that are probably more common than you might think. It's not just in science fiction movies anymore; AI is weaving its way into the fabric of our daily lives and various industries, often behind the scenes making things smoother, faster, and sometimes just plain smarter.

Think about when you pick up your smartphone. You're likely using AI in various ways without even realizing it. If you use facial recognition to unlock your phone, that's AI at work, identifying your unique features. When you use a voice assistant like Siri or Google Assistant to ask a question or set a reminder, that's Natural Language Processing (NLP), a branch of AI, understanding your speech and responding. Even your camera often uses AI to automatically focus, adjust settings, and even recognize scenes or objects in the frame.

Now, let's step away from your pocket and think about the internet and online services. When you use a search engine like Google, the results you see are heavily influenced by AI algorithms that try to understand what you're looking for and rank the most relevant pages. If you've ever noticed personalized recommendations on shopping sites like Amazon or streaming services like Netflix, that's AI analyzing your past behavior and suggesting things you might like. Even the way your social media feeds are curated, showing you posts and ads that the platform thinks you'll find interesting, is driven by AI. And those annoying spam filters in your email? Yep, that's AI working hard to keep your inbox clean.

The world of customer service has also been significantly impacted by AI. We've already mentioned voice assistants, but think about chatbots you might encounter on websites. These AI-powered programs can answer common questions, provide information, and guide you through processes, often handling a large volume of inquiries efficiently, 24/7. They're getting smarter all the time, understanding more complex questions and providing more helpful responses.

Transportation is another sector undergoing a massive AI-driven transformation. While fully self-driving cars are still evolving, AI is already present in many aspects of driving. Navigation apps use AI to analyze real-time traffic data and suggest the best routes. Features like adaptive cruise control and lane assist in modern cars rely on AI to perceive the environment and make driving adjustments. And the development of fully autonomous vehicles hinges on sophisticated AI systems that can understand complex driving scenarios and make safe decisions.

The healthcare industry is seeing a surge in AI applications. AI is being used to analyze medical images like X-rays and MRIs to help doctors detect diseases earlier. It's assisting in drug discovery by analyzing vast amounts of biological data to identify potential drug candidates. AI is also being used to personalize treatment plans based on a patient's individual characteristics and medical history. Even robotic surgery is becoming more prevalent, with AI playing a role in enhancing precision and control.

In the financial industry, AI is crucial for tasks like fraud detection, analyzing massive amounts of transaction data to identify suspicious patterns. It's also used for credit risk assessment, helping lenders make more informed decisions. Algorithmic trading in the stock market relies on AI to analyze market trends and execute trades at high speeds. And personalized financial advice is becoming more common, with AI systems helping people manage their money and make investment decisions.

Even in manufacturing, AI is playing an increasingly important role. Robots powered by AI are used for automation on assembly lines, performing repetitive tasks with high precision. Quality control is being improved with AI-powered vision systems that can inspect products for defects. And predictive maintenance uses AI to analyze sensor data from machinery to anticipate potential failures and schedule maintenance proactively, reducing downtime.

Think about how content is created and delivered. AI is being used in recommendation engines for music and video platforms. It's also being explored for content generation, with AI models now capable of writing articles, creating music, and even generating images. In advertising, AI helps to target ads to the people who are most likely to be interested in them.

Across all these applications, a key aspect of AI is its ability to analyze large amounts of data and find patterns that humans might miss. This allows for better predictions, more efficient processes, and more personalized experiences. AI is also continuously learning and improving as it is exposed to more data, making these applications increasingly sophisticated over time.

So, while you might not see a humanoid robot serving you coffee every day just yet, AI is already deeply embedded in many of the technologies and services we use regularly. It's a quiet revolution happening all around us, making things smarter and more efficient in ways that are often invisible but increasingly impactful.

Robotics

Alright, let's talk about something really cool that often goes hand-in-hand with Artificial Intelligence: Robotics. When you think of a robot, you might picture something from a science fiction movie – a shiny humanoid figure with blinking lights. While those kinds of robots might exist in the future, the reality of robotics today is much more diverse and incredibly fascinating. At its core, robotics is about designing, building, operating, and applying robots. And what exactly *is* a robot? Well, it's essentially a machine that can perform tasks autonomously, often with some level of intelligence or pre-programmed instructions.

Now, the history of robotics is longer than you might think. People have been dreaming about and even building automated devices for centuries, from simple mechanical toys to more complex automata. But the field really took off with the advent of modern computing and advancements in engineering and materials science.

A key aspect of a robot is its ability to interact with the physical world. This usually involves actuators, which are like the robot's muscles – motors, pistons, or other devices that allow it to move and manipulate things. It also involves sensors, which are like the robot's senses – cameras, touch sensors, proximity sensors, and more – that allow it to perceive its environment.

But a robot isn't just a collection of motors and sensors; it also needs a brain to control everything and make decisions. This is where the connection with AI becomes really strong. While some robots operate based on simple pre-programmed sequences of actions, many modern robots, especially those designed for more complex tasks, incorporate AI algorithms to enable them to be more autonomous, adaptable, and intelligent.

Think about a simple industrial robot arm on a car assembly line. It might be programmed to perform the same welding task over and over again, precisely and efficiently. That's robotics, but it might not involve a lot of sophisticated AI. However, consider a robot designed to navigate a warehouse, pick up specific items, and deliver them to different locations. This kind of robot needs to perceive its environment, understand instructions, plan its path, avoid obstacles, and maybe even recognize the items it needs to pick. That's where AI, particularly computer vision for recognizing objects and path planning algorithms, becomes essential.

Robotics is a really broad field, and robots come in all shapes, sizes, and capabilities, designed for a huge variety of applications.

In manufacturing, robots are workhorses, performing tasks like welding, painting, assembly, and packaging with incredible speed, precision, and consistency. They can work in hazardous environments and perform repetitive tasks tirelessly, increasing efficiency and quality.

In the healthcare industry, robots are being used for everything from assisting with surgery to delivering medication in hospitals and providing companionship to the elderly. Surgical robots can offer surgeons enhanced dexterity and precision, leading to less invasive procedures and faster recovery times.

Logistics and warehousing are also seeing a big increase in the use of robots. Autonomous mobile robots (AMRs) can navigate warehouses to transport goods, and robotic arms can automate tasks like picking and packing orders. This helps to streamline operations and reduce labor costs.

Exploration and hazardous environments are another key area for robotics. Robots can be sent into space to explore planets, into the deep sea to study marine life, or into disaster zones to search for survivors or handle dangerous materials. They can go where humans can't or where it's too risky for us to go.

Agriculture is starting to embrace robotics for tasks like planting seeds, harvesting crops, and monitoring plant health. This can lead to more efficient farming practices and increased yields.

Even in our homes, robots are becoming more common, from robotic vacuum cleaners that autonomously clean our floors to more advanced home assistants that can understand voice commands and control smart devices.

The field of human-robot interaction is also growing, focusing on designing robots that can work safely and effectively alongside humans. This includes developing robots with better sensing capabilities, more natural communication interfaces, and the ability to understand and respond to human emotions.

As AI continues to advance, we can expect robots to become even more intelligent, adaptable, and capable.

They will be able to perform more complex tasks, make more autonomous decisions, and interact with us in more natural and intuitive ways. From the factory floor to our homes, from exploring distant planets to assisting in delicate surgeries, robotics, powered by AI, is poised to play an increasingly significant role in shaping our future. It's about creating machines that can not only perform physical tasks but also think, learn, and adapt to the world around them.

Human-Robot Interaction and Autonomous Systems

Okay, let's delve into a really fascinating and increasingly important area: how humans and robots interact, and the rise of autonomous systems. You see, as robots become more capable and AI gets smarter, the way we work with and alongside these machines is evolving in some pretty significant ways. It's not just about robots replacing humans; it's also about creating partnerships where we can leverage the strengths of both.

When we talk about human-robot interaction (HRI), we're essentially looking at how people and robots communicate and work together. This can range from a person directly controlling a robot for a specific task to a robot operating more independently in a shared environment. The goal of HRI is to make these interactions safe, efficient, and even intuitive.

Think about some of the early industrial robots. They were often kept in cages for safety because they weren't designed to work closely with humans. Their movements were pre-programmed and they weren't very good at sensing or responding to unexpected changes in their environment, like a person suddenly stepping into their workspace.

But things are changing rapidly. Modern HRI is focusing on creating robots that can be more aware of their surroundings and the people they're working with. This involves equipping robots with better sensors – things like advanced cameras, depth sensors, and even force sensors that can tell if they've bumped into something or someone.

More importantly, it involves giving robots the "intelligence," often powered by AI, to understand human intent and respond appropriately. For example, if a person gestures towards an object, a collaborative robot might be able to understand that the person wants it to pick up that object. This kind of intuitive interaction requires sophisticated AI in areas like computer vision (to understand gestures and objects) and natural language processing (to understand spoken commands).

Another key aspect of HRI is safety. As robots start working more closely with humans, ensuring they don't cause harm is paramount. This involves designing robots with safety features like collision avoidance systems and force limits, as well as developing AI algorithms that can predict human behavior and react safely in dynamic environments. Imagine a robot working in a warehouse alongside human workers; it needs to be able to navigate without bumping into people and stop safely if someone gets too close.

Beyond just safety and basic task execution, HRI also looks at the social aspects of human-robot interaction. How do we build trust with robots? How can robots be designed to be more helpful and even feel more like partners? Researchers are exploring things like giving robots more expressive movements or even the ability to understand and respond to human emotions. While we're not quite at the level of having truly emotionally intelligent robots, these are active areas of investigation.

Now, let's shift gears a bit and talk about autonomous systems. An autonomous system is one that can operate independently without direct human control for extended periods or in complex environments. Think of a self-driving car navigating city streets, or a drone delivering packages, or even a robot exploring the surface of Mars. These systems rely heavily on AI to perceive their surroundings, plan their actions, and make decisions without constant human intervention.

The level of autonomy can vary. Some systems might require occasional human oversight, while others are designed to operate completely independently. Achieving true autonomy is a significant technical challenge, requiring robust AI in areas like perception (understanding the environment through sensors), planning (deciding what actions to take to achieve a goal), and control (executing those actions effectively).

Take a self-driving car again. It needs to perceive the world around it using cameras, lidar, and radar, identifying things like other vehicles, pedestrians, traffic lights, and road signs – that's the perception part, heavily reliant on computer vision and sensor fusion. Then, it needs to plan its route, decide when to accelerate, brake, or turn, and anticipate the actions of other road users – that's the planning and decision-making, often involving complex AI algorithms. Finally, it needs to control the vehicle's steering, acceleration, and braking systems to execute those plans smoothly and safely – that's the control aspect, which also often involves sophisticated software.

Autonomous systems are finding applications in a wide range of fields. In logistics, autonomous robots and drones can automate delivery and warehouse operations. In agriculture, autonomous tractors and harvesters can work around the clock to improve efficiency. In surveillance and security, autonomous drones can patrol large areas and identify potential threats. In exploration, autonomous robots can venture into dangerous or inaccessible environments.

The rise of autonomous systems also brings up important ethical and societal questions. Who is responsible when an autonomous system makes a mistake? How do we ensure these systems are fair and don't perpetuate biases? What are the implications for jobs and the workforce as more tasks become automated? These are complex issues that researchers, policymakers, and the public are actively grappling with.

Both human-robot interaction and autonomous systems are about finding the right balance between human capabilities and the potential of robots and AI. It's about creating systems that can augment human abilities, perform tasks that are dangerous or tedious for humans, and operate independently when needed, all while ensuring safety, efficiency, and ethical considerations are at the forefront. As AI continues to advance, the way we interact with and rely on these intelligent machines will only become more profound and integrated into our lives.

Chapter 5: Transformative Applications of AI

Alright, let's buckle up and take a deep dive into the world of Autonomous Vehicles, or self-driving cars as they're often called. This is a topic that's generating a lot of buzz, and for good reason – the idea of cars that can drive themselves seems like something straight out of science fiction, yet it's rapidly becoming a reality. Think about it: no more commuting stress, the ability to multitask or relax during your journey, and potentially safer roads. It's a pretty compelling vision, and AI is the engine making it all possible.

At its heart, an autonomous vehicle is a car that can operate without human intervention. This means it can perceive its surroundings, plan a route, and control its movement to reach a destination safely and efficiently, all on its own. Achieving this level of autonomy is an incredibly complex engineering and AI challenge, requiring a symphony of different technologies working together seamlessly.

One of the most crucial aspects of an autonomous vehicle is its ability to perceive the world around it. Just like we use our eyes, ears, and sense of touch to understand our environment while driving, self-driving cars rely on a suite of sensors to gather information. The most common types of sensors you'll find on these vehicles include cameras, which provide detailed visual information about the road, other vehicles, pedestrians, and traffic signals; radar, which uses radio waves to detect the distance and speed of objects, even in challenging weather conditions like fog or heavy rain; and lidar, which uses laser beams to create a high-resolution 3D map of the surroundings. Think of lidar as giving the car a very precise, point-by-point picture of everything around it. Some vehicles also use ultrasonic sensors, which are good for detecting nearby objects at lower speeds, like during parking.

The raw data from these sensors is just a stream of signals. This is where Artificial Intelligence, particularly Computer Vision and Sensor Fusion, comes into play. Computer vision algorithms analyze the images from the cameras to identify and classify objects – is that a car, a pedestrian, a bicycle, a stop sign? Sensor fusion is the process of combining the data from all the different sensors to create a comprehensive and reliable understanding of the environment. Each sensor has its strengths and weaknesses, and by fusing their data, the AI can get a more complete and accurate picture than any single sensor could provide on its own. For example, a camera might have trouble seeing in heavy fog, but radar can still detect moving objects.

Once the autonomous vehicle has a good understanding of its surroundings, the next step is planning its path. This involves determining the best route to the destination, taking into account things like traffic conditions, road closures, and speed limits. AI algorithms for path planning and decision-making are used to figure out the optimal course of action. This includes deciding when to accelerate, when to brake, when to turn, and how to navigate complex intersections.

The AI also needs to predict the behavior of other road users. This is a really challenging aspect, as it involves understanding human intentions. For example, if a pedestrian is looking like they might step into the road, the autonomous vehicle needs to anticipate that and react accordingly. This requires sophisticated AI models that can learn patterns of behavior from vast amounts of driving data.

The autonomous vehicle needs to control its movement – steering, acceleration, and braking – to execute the planned actions smoothly and safely. This involves sophisticated control systems that translate the AI's decisions into precise commands for the vehicle's mechanical components.

The development of autonomous vehicles is often described in terms of levels of autonomy, ranging from Level 0 (no automation, the human driver does everything) to Level 5 (full automation, the vehicle can handle all driving tasks in all conditions without human intervention). Currently, most commercially available vehicles with "autopilot" or similar features are at Level 2 or Level 3, meaning they can assist with certain driving tasks like steering and acceleration, but still require a human driver to be alert and ready to take over at any time. Achieving Level 4 and Level 5 autonomy is the ultimate goal, but it presents significant technical and regulatory challenges.

One of the biggest hurdles is ensuring safety. Autonomous vehicles need to be at least as safe as, if not safer than, human drivers, and they need to be able to handle a wide range of unexpected situations, from sudden obstacles in the road to adverse weather conditions. This requires rigorous testing and validation, often involving millions of miles of real-world and simulated driving.

Another challenge is dealing with edge cases – those rare but critical situations that a self-driving car might encounter. For example, how should an autonomous vehicle react to an emergency vehicle with flashing lights and sirens? How should it navigate in a construction zone with unusual lane markings? These scenarios require the AI to have a deep understanding of traffic laws and social driving norms.

Ethical considerations also play a significant role in the development of autonomous vehicles. For example, in an unavoidable accident scenario, if the car has to choose between two bad outcomes, how should it be programmed to decide? These are complex ethical dilemmas that need to be addressed.

Despite these challenges, the potential benefits of autonomous vehicles are enormous. They could lead to fewer accidents caused by human error, reduced traffic congestion through optimized routing and coordination, increased fuel efficiency through smoother driving, and greater mobility for people who are currently unable to drive.

The journey to fully autonomous vehicles is a marathon, not a sprint, but the progress made in recent years has been remarkable. As AI continues to advance and our understanding of the complexities of driving deepens, we are steadily moving closer to a future where self-driving cars are a common sight on our roads, promising to reshape transportation as we know it. It's a testament to the power of artificial intelligence to tackle some of the most challenging real-world problems.

How AI Drives Cars

Let's take a look at how Artificial Intelligence is the real brains behind a lot of the cool autonomous machines we're starting to see, from self-driving cars zipping around (well, trying to!) to drones soaring through the sky, and even other robotic systems operating in all sorts of environments. It's like giving these machines a digital pilot, a virtual navigator, and a decision-maker all rolled into one.

When we talk about self-driving cars, as we just discussed, AI is absolutely fundamental. It's not just about following a pre-programmed route; it's about perceiving the constantly changing environment in real-time, understanding what's happening, predicting what might happen next, and then making safe and efficient driving decisions. The AI system in an autonomous vehicle is like a highly skilled human driver, but instead of using eyes, ears, and intuition, it relies on a sophisticated array of sensors and powerful algorithms.

Think about how the AI "sees" the road. Cameras capture visual information, which is then processed by computer vision algorithms to identify objects like other cars, pedestrians, cyclists, traffic lights, and road signs. Radar and lidar sensors provide information about the distance and speed of these objects, even in conditions where cameras might struggle. The AI then fuses all this sensory data together to build a comprehensive understanding of the car's surroundings – a sort of real-time 3D map of everything nearby.

But just "seeing" isn't enough. The AI also needs to understand what it's seeing. For example, it needs to know that a red light means "stop," that a pedestrian might step into the road, and that another car's turn signal indicates it's about to change lanes. This involves complex AI models that have been trained on vast amounts of driving data to recognize patterns and predict behaviors.

Based on its understanding of the situation, the AI then needs to plan its actions. This involves deciding on the best route to follow, when to accelerate or brake, when to turn, and how to navigate intersections safely. Path planning algorithms and decision-making software work together to figure out the optimal course of action, taking into account traffic laws, road conditions, and the goals of the journey.

The AI needs to control the vehicle – sending commands to the steering wheel, the accelerator, and the brakes to execute its planned actions smoothly and precisely. This involves sophisticated control systems that translate the AI's decisions into physical movements of the car.

Now, let's take to the skies and talk about drones. AI is also a critical component in many modern drones, especially those that can operate autonomously. Just like self-driving cars, autonomous drones need to be able to perceive their environment, plan their flight paths, and control their movement.

For a drone, perception might involve cameras for visual navigation and object detection, GPS for location awareness, and inertial measurement units (IMUs) to understand its orientation and movement. AI algorithms, particularly in computer vision, allow drones to identify landmarks, avoid obstacles like trees or buildings, and even track moving objects.

Flight planning for autonomous drones can be quite complex, especially for tasks like package delivery or surveying large areas. AI algorithms are used to generate efficient flight paths, taking into account factors like battery life, wind conditions, and no-fly zones.

Control systems in drones use AI to maintain stable flight, follow planned paths accurately, and respond to changes in the environment. Some advanced drones can even perform complex maneuvers autonomously.

Beyond cars and drones, AI is also driving a wide range of other autonomous systems. Think about robots in warehouses that can navigate and pick items without human guidance. These robots use AI for tasks like mapping their environment, recognizing objects, and planning efficient routes.

In agriculture, autonomous robots are being developed to perform tasks like planting, weeding, and harvesting crops. These robots use AI-powered vision systems to identify plants, detect weeds, and navigate fields.

Even in underwater exploration, autonomous underwater vehicles (AUVs) use AI to navigate the deep sea, map the ocean floor, and collect data without human intervention.

The common thread across all these applications is that AI provides the "intelligence" that allows these machines to operate independently. It enables them to perceive their surroundings, understand complex situations, make decisions, and control their actions to achieve specific goals.

The level of autonomy can vary greatly depending on the application and the current state of the technology. Some systems might require a significant amount of human oversight, while others can operate with very little or no human intervention. As AI continues to advance, we can expect to see even more sophisticated and capable autonomous systems emerging in all sorts of domains, changing the way we live, work, and interact with technology. It's about giving machines the ability to navigate and operate intelligently in the real world, extending our reach and capabilities in countless ways.

Virtual Assistants and Smart Devices

Okay, let's take a look at how Artificial Intelligence is the real brains behind a lot of the cool autonomous machines we're starting to see, from self-driving cars zipping around (well, trying to!) to drones soaring through the sky, and even other robotic systems operating in all sorts of environments. It's like giving these machines a digital pilot, a virtual navigator, and a decision-maker all rolled into one.

When we talk about self-driving cars, as we just discussed, AI is absolutely fundamental. It's not just about following a pre-programmed route; it's about perceiving the constantly changing environment in real-time, understanding what's happening, predicting what might happen next, and then making safe and efficient driving decisions. The AI system in an autonomous vehicle is like a highly skilled human driver, but instead of using eyes, ears, and intuition, it relies on a sophisticated array of sensors and powerful algorithms.

Think about how the AI "sees" the road. Cameras capture visual information, which is then processed by computer vision algorithms to identify objects like other cars, pedestrians, cyclists, traffic lights, and road signs. Radar and lidar sensors provide information about the distance and speed of these objects, even in conditions where cameras might struggle. The AI then fuses all this sensory data together to build a comprehensive understanding of the car's surroundings – a sort of real-time 3D map of everything nearby.

But just "seeing" isn't enough. The AI also needs to understand what it's seeing. For example, it needs to know that a red light means "stop," that a pedestrian might step into the road, and that another car's turn signal indicates it's about to change lanes. This involves complex AI models that have been trained on vast amounts of driving data to recognize patterns and predict behaviors.

Based on its understanding of the situation, the AI then needs to plan its actions. This involves deciding on the best route to follow, when to accelerate or brake, when to turn, and how to navigate intersections safely. Path planning algorithms and decision-making software work together to figure out the optimal course of action, taking into account traffic laws, road conditions, and the goals of the journey.

The AI needs to control the vehicle – sending commands to the steering wheel, the accelerator, and the brakes to execute its planned actions smoothly and precisely. This involves sophisticated control systems that translate the AI's decisions into physical movements of the car.

Now, let's take to the skies and talk about drones. AI is also a critical component in many modern drones, especially those that can operate autonomously. Just like self-driving cars, autonomous drones need to be able to perceive their environment, plan their flight paths, and control their movement.

For a drone, perception might involve cameras for visual navigation and object detection, GPS for location awareness, and inertial measurement units (IMUs) to understand its orientation and movement. AI algorithms, particularly in computer vision, allow drones to identify landmarks, avoid obstacles like trees or buildings, and even track moving objects.

Flight planning for autonomous drones can be quite complex, especially for tasks like package delivery or surveying large areas. AI algorithms are used to generate efficient flight paths, taking into account factors like battery life, wind conditions, and no-fly zones.

Control systems in drones use AI to maintain stable flight, follow planned paths accurately, and respond to changes in the environment. Some advanced drones can even perform complex maneuvers autonomously.

Beyond cars and drones, AI is also driving a wide range of other autonomous systems. Think about robots in warehouses that can navigate and pick items without human guidance. These robots use AI for tasks like mapping their environment, recognizing objects, and planning efficient routes.

In agriculture, autonomous robots are being developed to perform tasks like planting, weeding, and harvesting crops. These robots use AI-powered vision systems to identify plants, detect weeds, and navigate fields.

Even in underwater exploration, autonomous underwater vehicles (AUVs) use AI to navigate the deep sea, map the ocean floor, and collect data without human intervention.

The common thread across all these applications is that AI provides the "intelligence" that allows these machines to operate independently. It enables them to perceive their surroundings, understand complex situations, make decisions, and control their actions to achieve specific goals.

The level of autonomy can vary greatly depending on the application and the current state of the technology. Some systems might require a significant amount of human oversight, while others can operate with very little or no human intervention. As AI continues to advance, we can expect to see even more sophisticated and capable autonomous systems emerging in all sorts of domains, changing the way we live, work, and interact with technology. It's about giving machines the ability to navigate and operate intelligently in the real world, extending our reach and capabilities in countless ways.

Alexa, Siri, and Google Assistant

Now, let's pull back the curtain on those helpful voices in our homes and pockets – Alexa, Siri, and Google Assistant. You probably chat with them to play music, set timers, or ask about the weather, and it might seem like magic. But behind those seemingly simple interactions is a fascinating array of technologies, powered by Artificial Intelligence, working together to understand you and respond. Think of it like a really complex, multi-talented assistant who's always ready to help.

The first crucial step in making these voice assistants work is speech recognition, which is the ability for the device to hear what you're saying and convert those sounds into digital text. This is a surprisingly challenging task because human speech is so variable. We all have different accents, speaking speeds, and pronunciations. There's background noise, coughs, and stutters to contend with. To tackle this, these assistants use sophisticated acoustic models that have been trained on massive amounts of audio data of people speaking in all sorts of conditions. These models learn to identify the basic sound units of language (phonemes) and then string them together to form words. Deep learning, particularly using recurrent neural networks and transformer networks, has significantly improved the accuracy of speech recognition, making these assistants much better at understanding what we say, even when we're not speaking perfectly clearly.

Once the device has transcribed your speech into text, the next big challenge is Natural Language Understanding (NLU). This is where the AI tries to figure out what you actually *mean* by what you said. It's not just about recognizing the words; it's about understanding the intent behind them. For example, if you say "Play some jazz music," the assistant needs to understand that "play" is a command, "jazz music" is the desired action, and it needs to initiate the process of finding and playing that music.

NLU involves several steps. First, the system needs to parse the sentence, breaking it down into its grammatical components to understand the structure. Then, it needs to understand the meaning of the individual words, often using techniques like word embeddings that we talked about before, where words with similar meanings are represented in a way that the AI can recognize their relationship. But crucially, NLU also needs to understand the context of your request. If you've just asked about the weather in O'Fallon and then say "How about tomorrow?", the assistant needs to understand that "tomorrow" refers to the weather in O'Fallon, not somewhere else.

Another important part of NLU is intent recognition. The AI needs to figure out what you're trying to achieve with your request. Are you trying to play music, set a timer, ask a question, or control a smart home device? This involves classifying your utterance into one of many possible intents. For example, "Turn on the living room lights" and "Switch on the lamp" have different wording but the same underlying intent: to control a light.

Once the assistant has understood your intent, it often needs to extract specific pieces of information from your request, called entities. For example, if you say "Set a timer for 20 minutes," the intent is to set a timer, and the entity is "20 minutes." If you ask "What's the weather in

O'Fallon?", the intent is to get the weather, and the entity is "O'Fallon." Identifying these entities allows the assistant to perform the correct action with the right parameters.

After understanding your request, the assistant needs to figure out how to respond. This involves dialogue management, which is like managing a conversation. The assistant needs to keep track of the conversation history, understand follow-up questions, and decide what to say next to be helpful. For example, if you ask for the weather and then say "What about the humidity?", the assistant needs to remember the context of your initial weather query.

The assistant needs to generate a response. This could be as simple as providing information it has readily available (like the current time) or it might involve taking an action and then confirming it (like saying "Okay, I've set a timer for 20 minutes"). If the response involves spoken language, it goes through the process of text-to-speech (TTS), which converts the digital text back into natural-sounding speech. Modern TTS systems use advanced techniques to generate speech that sounds very human-like, with natural intonation and rhythm.

So, when you interact with Alexa, Siri, or Google Assistant, it seems like a simple back-and-forth, but behind the scenes, a complex pipeline of AI technologies is working in concert. Speech recognition turns your words into text, NLU figures out what you mean, dialogue management keeps track of the conversation, and text-to-speech generates the response. All of this is powered by vast amounts of data and sophisticated machine learning models that are constantly being refined to make these assistants more accurate, more helpful, and more natural to interact with. It's a testament to how far AI has come in understanding and responding to the complexities of human language.

Predictive Analytics

Let's talk about something really useful and increasingly common in the world today: Predictive Analytics. Now, the name might sound a bit technical, but at its heart, it's really about using data and statistical techniques, often powered by Artificial Intelligence and Machine Learning, to figure out what's likely to happen in the future. Think of it like being able to make pretty good guesses about what's coming down the road, based on what's happened in the past.

We humans do this all the time in our daily lives, even if we don't call it "predictive analytics." For example, if you see dark clouds gathering, you might predict that it's going to rain and decide to take an umbrella. You're using past experience (dark clouds often lead to rain) to make a prediction about the future. Predictive analytics for businesses and organizations works on a similar principle, but on a much larger scale and with more sophisticated tools.

At its core, predictive analytics involves looking at historical data, identifying patterns and trends, and then building models that can extrapolate those patterns into the future to forecast what's likely to occur. It's like a detective looking at clues from the past to solve a future crime, but instead of crimes, we're often predicting things like customer behavior, market trends, or potential risks.

The process typically starts with data. Just like a detective needs evidence, predictive analytics needs a solid foundation of relevant and high-quality data. This data can come from all sorts of sources – sales records, website activity, social media data, sensor readings, financial transactions, you name it. The more relevant and comprehensive the data, the better the predictions are likely to be.

Once the data is gathered, the next step is data preparation. This involves cleaning the data (removing errors or inconsistencies), transforming it into a usable format, and often selecting the most relevant features or variables that might influence the outcome we're trying to predict. Think of it like organizing all the clues and highlighting the ones that seem most important.

Then comes the crucial part: building the predictive model. This is where various statistical and machine learning techniques come into play. We talked about some of these earlier, like regression (for predicting continuous values like sales figures) and classification (for predicting categories like whether a customer will churn or not). The choice of which model to use depends on the type of data we have and what we're trying to predict.

For example, if we want to predict how many units of a product we'll sell next month, we might use a time series forecasting model that looks at past sales trends and seasonality. If we want to predict which customers are most likely to stop using our service, we might use a classification model that analyzes their past behavior and identifies patterns associated with churn.

Once a model is built, it needs to be trained using the historical data. The algorithm learns the relationships between the input variables and the outcome we're trying to predict. It's like the detective learning to recognize patterns in past crimes that might indicate a future one.

After training, the model needs to be evaluated to see how accurate its predictions are. We typically use a separate set of data that the model hasn't seen before to test its performance. This helps us to understand how well the model is likely to perform on new, real-world data.

If the model performs well, it can then be deployed to make predictions on new data. For example, a deployed model might continuously analyze customer data and flag those who are at high risk of leaving, allowing the company to take proactive steps to retain them.

The applications of predictive analytics are incredibly wide-ranging across various industries.

In business, it's used for things like customer relationship management (CRM) to predict customer churn, identify cross-selling and upselling opportunities, and personalize marketing campaigns. It's also used in supply chain management to forecast demand, optimize inventory levels, and predict potential disruptions. In finance, it's used for risk management, predicting credit defaults and detecting fraudulent transactions.

In healthcare, predictive analytics can help identify patients who are at high risk of developing certain diseases, predict hospital readmissions, and optimize resource allocation.

In retail, it's used to forecast sales, optimize pricing, and personalize product recommendations.

Even in sports, predictive analytics is used to forecast game outcomes and player performance.

The power of predictive analytics lies in its ability to help organizations make more informed decisions, anticipate future challenges and opportunities, and ultimately operate more efficiently and effectively. By leveraging the vast amounts of data available today and using sophisticated analytical techniques, we can gain valuable insights into what the future might hold and take proactive steps to shape it. It's like having a crystal ball, but one that's based on data and rigorous analysis rather than magic. And as AI and machine learning continue to advance, the accuracy and sophistication of predictive analytics will only continue to grow, making it an even more indispensable tool in the years to come.

Forecasting Trends and Decision Making

Next, let's talk about how Artificial Intelligence is becoming a real game-changer when it comes to figuring out what might happen in the future – forecasting trends – and then using those predictions to make smarter decisions. Think of it like having a super-powered crystal ball that's not based on magic, but on analyzing tons and tons of data to spot patterns and make informed guesses about what's coming next. And then, using those guesses to guide our choices.

We humans have always tried to predict the future, from ancient astrologers looking at the stars to modern economists analyzing market data. But AI brings a whole new level of power and sophistication to this process. It can sift through massive datasets that would be impossible for a human to process, identify subtle relationships and correlations, and build complex models to make predictions with increasing accuracy.

When it comes to forecasting trends, AI uses a variety of techniques, often falling under the umbrella of predictive analytics, which we just talked about. One common approach is time series analysis. Imagine you have a long history of sales data for a particular product. AI algorithms can analyze this data, looking for patterns like seasonal fluctuations, long-term growth trends, and cyclical behaviors. By understanding these patterns, the AI can then extrapolate them into the future to forecast how sales might look in the coming weeks, months, or even years. This is incredibly useful for businesses to plan inventory, production, and marketing efforts.

Beyond just sales, AI can be used to forecast all sorts of trends. In finance, it can analyze market data, economic indicators, and even news sentiment to try and predict stock prices or identify emerging investment opportunities. In healthcare, AI can analyze patient data to forecast disease outbreaks or predict which patients are at high risk of developing certain conditions. In energy, it can forecast energy demand based on weather patterns and usage trends. Even in social media, AI can analyze vast amounts of posts and interactions to identify emerging trends in public opinion or viral topics.

The key advantage of AI in forecasting is its ability to handle complex, non-linear relationships in the data. Traditional statistical methods often struggle with these kinds of complexities, but machine learning algorithms can learn intricate patterns that might be invisible to the human eye. For example, AI might discover that a seemingly unrelated factor, like the weather in a different part of the world, actually has a subtle but significant impact on the sales of a particular product.

Now, forecasting trends is only half the battle. The real value comes when we use those predictions to make better decisions. This is where AI truly shines as a decision-support tool. By providing us with insights into what's likely to happen, AI can help us to make more informed choices and mitigate risks or capitalize on opportunities.

Think about a retail business using AI to forecast demand for different products. If the AI predicts a surge in demand for a particular item in the coming weeks, the business can proactively increase its inventory levels to avoid stockouts and potentially miss out on sales. Conversely, if the AI predicts a decline in demand for another product, the business can reduce its orders and potentially offer discounts to clear out existing stock.

In finance, if AI predicts a potential downturn in a particular market, investors might choose to adjust their portfolios to reduce their exposure to risk. If AI identifies a promising new investment trend, they might decide to allocate more capital to that area.

In healthcare, if AI predicts that a patient is at high risk of a certain complication after surgery, doctors can take preventive measures to reduce that risk. If AI forecasts a flu outbreak in a specific region, public health officials can launch targeted vaccination campaigns.

The role of AI in decision-making often involves not just providing a single prediction, but also offering insights into the factors driving that prediction and even suggesting potential actions. For example, an AI system might not just predict that a customer is likely to churn, but also identify the specific behaviors or interactions that are contributing to that risk, allowing the company to address those issues proactively.

AI can help us to evaluate different potential decisions by simulating their likely outcomes based on the forecasted trends. This allows us to compare different strategies and choose the one that is most likely to lead to the desired results. For example, a marketing team might use AI to simulate the potential impact of different advertising campaigns on sales before launching them, allowing them to choose the most effective approach.

It's important to remember that AI is a tool to augment human decision-making, not to replace it entirely. While AI can provide valuable insights and predictions, human judgment, experience, and ethical considerations are still crucial in the decision-making process. The best approach is often a collaboration between humans and AI, where we leverage the strengths of both to make the most informed and effective choices.

As AI continues to evolve and become more sophisticated, its role in forecasting trends and informing our decisions will only become more significant. It has the potential to help us navigate an increasingly complex world with greater foresight and make choices that lead to better outcomes in all aspects of our lives and our organizations. It's like having a powerful assistant that can analyze the past, understand the present, and offer valuable guidance for the future.

Healthcare Innovations

So, let's step into a world where technology is becoming an increasingly vital partner in keeping us healthy: the realm of AI Healthcare Innovations. Now, when you think of healthcare, you probably picture doctors, nurses, hospitals, and maybe some high-tech equipment. But quietly, behind the scenes, Artificial Intelligence is starting to play a significant role, promising to revolutionize everything from how we diagnose diseases to how we receive treatment and manage our well-being. It's like having a super-smart assistant that can help doctors be even better, catch illnesses earlier, and personalize care in ways we never thought possible.

One of the most exciting areas where AI is making waves in healthcare is in medical imaging. Think about X-rays, MRIs, CT scans – these generate a huge amount of visual data that doctors need to analyze to find signs of illness. AI algorithms, particularly those based on computer vision (which we talked about earlier), are becoming incredibly adept at analyzing these images. They can be trained on vast datasets of scans, learning to identify subtle patterns and anomalies that might be easily missed by the human eye. For example, AI can help radiologists detect tiny tumors in mammograms, identify fractures in X-rays with greater accuracy, or even spot early signs of eye diseases in retinal scans.

This not only speeds up the diagnostic process but can also lead to earlier detection of serious conditions, which can significantly improve treatment outcomes.

Beyond just looking at static images, AI is also being used to analyze dynamic medical data, like the signals from an ECG monitoring your heart or the readings from wearable devices tracking your vital signs. By continuously monitoring this data and looking for unusual patterns, AI can help doctors detect potential problems early on, sometimes even before the patient experiences any symptoms. Imagine a system that can predict an impending heart event based on subtle changes in your heart rhythm detected by a smartwatch – that's the kind of proactive healthcare AI can enable.

Another really promising application of AI in healthcare is in disease diagnosis and treatment. AI algorithms can analyze a patient's medical history, genetic information, lifestyle factors, and current symptoms to help doctors arrive at more accurate diagnoses, sometimes even for complex or rare conditions. It's like having a super-knowledgeable consultant who has access to a vast library of medical information and can quickly sift through it to find the most likely explanation for a patient's illness.

AI is playing a role in personalized medicine. By analyzing the unique characteristics of each patient, including their genetic makeup and how they've responded to past treatments, AI can help doctors tailor treatment plans that are most likely to be effective for that individual. This moves away from a one-size-fits-all approach and towards more precise and targeted therapies, potentially leading to better outcomes and fewer side effects. For example, in cancer treatment, AI can help identify which specific drugs are most likely to work for a patient based on the genetic profile of their tumor.

AI is also making a big difference in drug discovery and development. Traditionally, finding new drugs is a long, expensive, and often hit-or-miss process. AI can speed up this process significantly by analyzing vast databases of biological and chemical information to identify potential drug candidates and predict how they might interact with the human body. This can help researchers narrow down their focus and accelerate the development of new and more effective treatments for various diseases.

Let's not forget the impact of AI on patient care and management. AI-powered virtual assistants and chatbots can help patients manage their medications, schedule appointments, and get answers to common health-related questions. They can also provide reminders for important health tasks and monitor patients remotely, alerting healthcare providers if there are any concerning changes in their condition. This can empower patients to take a more active role in their own care and free up healthcare professionals to focus on more complex cases.

Even in the administrative side of healthcare, AI is proving to be incredibly useful. It can automate tasks like processing insurance claims, scheduling appointments, and managing medical records, freeing up healthcare staff from these time-consuming activities and allowing them to dedicate more time to direct patient care.

Of course, the integration of AI into healthcare is not without its challenges. Issues around data privacy, security, and the ethical use of AI are crucial and need to be carefully addressed. It's important to ensure that these technologies are used responsibly and in a way that benefits everyone.

However, the potential of AI to transform healthcare is immense. From earlier and more accurate diagnoses to personalized treatments and more efficient care delivery, AI is poised to usher in a new era of medicine that is more precise, proactive, and patient-centered. It's like having a powerful new tool in the doctor's toolkit, one that can help them see more clearly, understand more deeply, and ultimately provide better care for all of us.

Diagnostics, Personalized Medicine, and Drug Discovery

Alright, let's really zoom in on three particularly exciting and transformative areas where Artificial Intelligence is making significant strides in healthcare: diagnostics, personalized medicine, and drug discovery. Think of these as three key pillars of modern healthcare that are being fundamentally reshaped by the power of AI, promising to make our healthcare systems more accurate, more tailored, and more efficient in the fight against disease.

First up, let's talk about diagnostics. This is the crucial first step in healthcare – figuring out what's wrong. Traditionally, this relies heavily on a doctor's expertise, their ability to interpret symptoms, analyze test results, and sometimes look at medical images. Now, AI is stepping in as a powerful ally in this process, offering the potential for faster, more accurate, and even earlier diagnoses.

Imagine a doctor looking at an X-ray to find a tiny fracture. It can be challenging, and sometimes subtle signs might be missed. But AI algorithms, especially those trained in computer vision, can be fed vast amounts of medical images – millions of X-rays with and without fractures – and learn to identify even the faintest indicators of a problem. They can highlight areas of concern that a human might overlook, leading to earlier and more accurate diagnoses. This isn't about replacing doctors; it's about giving them a super-powered second pair of eyes, one that has seen countless examples and can process images with incredible speed and precision.

The same principle applies to other medical imaging techniques like MRIs, CT scans, and retinal scans. AI can analyze these complex images to detect early signs of diseases like cancer, Alzheimer's, and diabetic retinopathy, often before symptoms even become apparent. Early detection is crucial for many conditions, as it can significantly improve the chances of successful treatment.

Beyond imaging, AI is also being used to analyze other types of diagnostic data. Think about blood tests, genetic information, and even the notes a doctor takes during an examination. AI algorithms, particularly those using natural language processing (NLP), can sift through these vast amounts of data, looking for patterns and correlations that might point to a specific diagnosis. For example, AI could analyze a patient's history of symptoms, combined with their genetic predispositions and the results of various tests, to suggest the most likely diagnosis or even flag rare conditions that might not be immediately obvious.

Now, let's move on to personalized medicine. This is the idea of tailoring medical treatment to the individual characteristics of each patient. We're all unique, with different genetic makeups, lifestyles, and responses to treatments. What works well for one person might not work as well for another. AI is playing a key role in making personalized medicine a reality.

By analyzing a patient's genomic data, AI can help doctors understand their individual predispositions to certain diseases and predict how they might respond to different therapies. For example, in cancer treatment, AI can analyze the genetic profile of a patient's tumor to identify specific mutations that might make it more susceptible to certain drugs. This allows doctors to choose the most targeted and effective treatments, minimizing side effects and improving outcomes.

AI is also being used to integrate various other types of patient data – from their medical history and lifestyle to information from wearable devices that track their activity levels and vital signs. By analyzing this holistic view of the patient, AI can help create highly personalized treatment plans, predict potential risks, and even suggest lifestyle modifications that could improve their health. Imagine an AI system that constantly monitors a patient with diabetes, predicting potential blood sugar spikes based on their diet and activity, and then providing personalized recommendations in real-time.

Let's talk about drug discovery. This is a notoriously long and expensive process. Traditionally, scientists would spend years screening thousands of compounds to find potential drug candidates, and even then, the success rate was low. AI is revolutionizing this process by making it faster, more efficient, and more targeted.

AI algorithms can analyze vast databases of biological and chemical information to identify potential drug targets – specific molecules in the body that are involved in disease. They can then screen millions of existing and potential drug compounds to predict which ones are most likely to interact with these targets in a beneficial way. This in silico (computer-based) screening can significantly narrow down the number of compounds that need to be tested in the lab, saving time and resources.

AI can help predict the safety and efficacy of potential drugs by analyzing data from previous clinical trials and understanding how different molecules interact with biological systems. This can help identify potential side effects early in the development process and increase the likelihood of a drug successfully making it through clinical trials.

AI is even being used in de novo drug design, where algorithms are used to generate entirely new molecules with specific properties that are predicted to be effective against a particular disease target. It's like having an AI chemist that can design novel drugs from scratch.

The impact of AI on diagnostics, personalized medicine, and drug discovery is still in its early stages, but the potential is enormous. It promises to make healthcare more precise, more proactive, and ultimately more effective in helping us live longer and healthier lives. By leveraging the power of data and intelligent algorithms, AI is becoming an indispensable tool in the ongoing quest to understand and combat disease.

AI in Entertainment and Media

Okay, let's dim the lights and cue the sound – we're diving into the fascinating world of AI in Entertainment and Media. Now, you might think of AI as something strictly technical, crunching numbers and powering robots. But it's also becoming a surprisingly creative force, changing how we make, distribute, and even experience movies, music, games, and all sorts of other media. Think of it as giving artists and storytellers a whole new set of tools, and even becoming a bit of a creative partner itself.

One of the most visible ways AI is impacting entertainment is through recommendation systems. If you've ever binged a new series on Netflix or discovered a new favorite song on Spotify, chances are AI was involved. These platforms use algorithms to analyze your viewing or listening history, your preferences, and even what other people with similar tastes enjoy. It's like having a super-knowledgeable friend who knows exactly what kind of movie you'd be in the mood for on a Friday night or what kind of music would get you through your workout. This not only makes it easier for us to find content we love but also helps creators reach wider audiences.

But AI's role goes way beyond just suggesting what to watch or listen to next. It's also getting into the creation process itself. Think about music. We're starting to see AI that can compose original music in various styles. You can give it a prompt – say, "a melancholic piano piece" – and it can generate something unique. While it might not replace human composers entirely, it can be a powerful tool for artists to experiment with new sounds, overcome creative blocks, or even create background scores for videos and games more efficiently.

The world of video games is also being heavily influenced by AI. For a long time, the non-player characters (NPCs) in games often followed very predictable patterns. But now, AI is making them much more intelligent and responsive. Imagine playing a game where the enemies learn from your tactics, adapt their behavior, and feel more like real opponents. AI is also being used to generate game worlds and storylines procedurally, meaning the game can create new content on the fly, making each playthrough feel fresh and unique. Think of vast, explorable worlds that are partly designed by algorithms, offering endless possibilities.

Even in filmmaking and video production, AI is starting to make its mark. It can assist with tasks like video editing, color correction, and even generating special effects. Imagine AI tools that can automatically remove unwanted objects from a scene or even create realistic-looking crowds. While we're not quite at the point of AI writing and directing entire feature films (though some experiments are happening!), it's becoming a valuable assistant in the production pipeline, potentially saving time and resources.

Another area where AI is making a difference is in content generation for marketing and advertising. AI tools can analyze trends and audience data to help create more effective ad copy, social media posts, and even video scripts. It's like having an AI marketing assistant that can help craft messages that are more likely to resonate with specific audiences.

Think about dubbing and subtitling. AI is being used to automatically translate and generate subtitles and dubbing in multiple languages, making content more accessible to a global audience. While it's not always perfect, it's rapidly improving and can significantly speed up the process of internationalizing media.

AI is also playing a role in analyzing audience reactions. By using techniques like sentiment analysis on social media and online comments, media companies can get a better understanding of how their content is being received, identify what's working and what's not, and make data-driven decisions about future projects.

Now, it's important to remember that AI in entertainment and media is still a developing field. There are ongoing discussions about the role of human creativity versus AI-generated content, questions about copyright and ownership, and the potential impact on artists and creators. It's a dynamic landscape, with new possibilities and challenges emerging all the time.

However, the potential for AI to enhance and transform the entertainment and media we consume is undeniable. It's about giving creators new tools, personalizing our experiences, and even opening up entirely new forms of entertainment that we can't even imagine yet. It's like a new act has entered the stage, and the show is just beginning.

AI-Generated Content, Recommendation Systems, and Gaming

Let's dive into three really exciting areas where Artificial Intelligence is shaking things up: AI-generated content, those clever recommendation systems that seem to know you better than you know yourself sometimes, and the ever-evolving world of gaming. You might not always realize it, but AI is playing an increasingly significant role in how we create, discover, and experience these things. Think of it as a new wave of creativity and personalization powered by smart algorithms.

First up, let's talk about AI-generated content. This might sound a bit futuristic, like robots taking over artistic expression, but it's already happening in some fascinating ways. At its core, it's about using AI algorithms to create things that traditionally required human input – things like text, music, images, and even videos.

Take text generation, for example. We're seeing AI models that can write articles, create product descriptions, generate social media posts, and even draft creative writing like poems or scripts. These models learn patterns and styles from massive amounts of text data and can then produce new content that often sounds surprisingly human-like. While it might not replace human writers entirely, it can be a powerful tool for brainstorming ideas, automating repetitive writing tasks, or even creating personalized content at scale. Imagine an AI that can generate tailored news summaries based on your interests or create unique marketing copy for different customer segments.

Then there's music generation. As we touched on before, AI can now compose original music in various genres. You can give it parameters like style, tempo, and mood, and it can create unique musical pieces. This can be useful for creating background music for videos or games, providing artists with new sonic palettes to explore, or even generating personalized music tailored to your listening preferences or activities.

Image generation is another rapidly advancing field. AI models can now create photorealistic images of objects, scenes, and even people that don't exist. You can give it a textual description – say, "a futuristic cityscape at sunset" – and it can generate a corresponding image. This has huge implications for art, design, and even creating visual content for marketing and entertainment.

We're even seeing AI venture into video generation, although this is still a more complex area. Imagine being able to describe a scene and have AI generate a short video clip of it. While still in its early stages, this could revolutionize filmmaking, animation, and content creation.

Now, let's shift gears and talk about recommendation systems. These are the algorithms that power those "You might also like..." sections on streaming services, online stores, and social media platforms. They're designed to predict what content or products you'll be most interested in based on your past behavior, your stated preferences, and the behavior of other users with similar tastes.

Think about how they work. They collect data about your interactions – what movies you've watched, what songs you've listened to, what products you've bought or browsed. Then, they use machine learning algorithms to find patterns in this data and identify similarities between you and other users. If people who liked the same movies you did also enjoyed a particular new series, the system might recommend that series to you.

Recommendation systems are becoming increasingly sophisticated, taking into account not just what you've liked in the past but also factors like the time of day, your current mood (sometimes inferred from your activity), and even what's currently trending. They're designed to keep you engaged and help you discover new things you might not have found otherwise. This is a win-win for both users, who get more personalized experiences, and for content creators and businesses, who can reach more relevant audiences.

Let's step into the exciting world of gaming. AI has been a part of games for a long time, primarily to control non-player characters (NPCs). But modern AI is taking gaming to a whole new level.

We're seeing more intelligent and adaptive NPCs. Instead of just following pre-programmed scripts, AI-powered NPCs can learn from the player's behavior, react more realistically to in-game events, and even exhibit more believable personalities. This can make games feel more immersive and challenging. Imagine enemies that coordinate their attacks or characters that remember your past interactions and respond accordingly.

AI is also being used for procedural content generation in games. This means that the game world, levels, items, and even storylines can be generated automatically by algorithms, rather than being entirely designed by humans. This can lead to vast, virtually endless game worlds and unique experiences every time you play. Think of open-world games that feel truly limitless or rogue-like games with constantly shifting environments.

AI is also enhancing the gameplay experience in other ways. It can be used for things like dynamic difficulty adjustment, where the game adapts its challenge based on your skill level, ensuring that it's always engaging but not too frustrating. AI can also be used to create more realistic physics simulations and more believable virtual environments.

AI is even being explored in areas like game design and testing. Algorithms can analyze game data to identify potential balance issues, find bugs, and even suggest improvements to the game design based on player behavior patterns.

So, from creating new forms of art and entertainment to helping us discover content we love and making our games more immersive and dynamic, AI is becoming an increasingly powerful and versatile force in the world of entertainment and media. It's about augmenting human creativity, personalizing our experiences, and opening up new possibilities for how we create, consume, and interact with the media we enjoy.

Chapter 6: Ethical Considerations

So, let's settle in and have a good, thoughtful chat about something that's going to touch pretty much every aspect of our lives in the coming years: the Societal Impacts of AI. Now, AI isn't just some abstract technology confined to labs and science fiction movies. It's starting to weave its way into the fabric of our society, and it's going to bring about some pretty big changes, both exciting and potentially challenging. Think of it like a powerful new force entering the world, and we need to understand how it's going to reshape things.

One of the most significant areas of impact is going to be on work and the economy. AI has the potential to automate many tasks that are currently done by humans, from repetitive manual labor in factories to more white-collar jobs like data entry and even some aspects of customer service. This could lead to increased efficiency and productivity, which could be great for the economy overall. Imagine a world where tedious and dangerous jobs are handled by robots, freeing up humans for more creative and fulfilling work.

However, this also raises important questions about employment. If machines can do many of the jobs that people currently rely on, what will happen to those workers? We might see a need for new kinds of jobs that focus on designing, building, maintaining, and managing

AI systems. There could also be a greater emphasis on uniquely human skills like creativity, critical thinking, emotional intelligence, and complex problem-solving. It's likely we'll need to think carefully about education, training, and social safety nets to help people adapt to these changes in the job market.

Another huge area of impact is healthcare. We've already talked about how AI is revolutionizing diagnostics, personalized medicine, and drug discovery. But think about the broader societal implications. AI could lead to earlier detection of diseases, more effective treatments tailored to individuals, and even new ways of preventing illnesses. This could mean longer, healthier lives for many people and a more efficient healthcare system overall. Imagine AI helping to manage chronic conditions remotely, providing personalized support and reducing the burden on hospitals and clinics. However, we also need to consider issues like access to these AI-powered healthcare technologies and ensuring that they are fair and unbiased for everyone.

Education is another sector ripe for transformation. AI could personalize learning experiences for students, tailoring the curriculum and pace to their individual needs and learning styles. Imagine AI tutors that can provide customized feedback and support, helping students master concepts at their own speed. AI could also automate administrative tasks for teachers, freeing them up to spend more time interacting with students. However, we need to think about how to ensure that AI in education complements human interaction and doesn't lead to a dehumanized learning experience.

Transportation is already being heavily impacted by AI with the development of autonomous vehicles. Imagine a future with fewer traffic accidents, more efficient traffic flow, and potentially lower transportation costs. AI-powered ride-sharing and delivery services could also become more widespread. However, we also need to consider the societal implications of job displacement for truck drivers and taxi drivers, as well as the ethical dilemmas that might arise in autonomous driving scenarios.

Even in criminal justice, AI is being used for things like predictive policing and risk assessment. While the goal is often to make the system more efficient and reduce bias, there are serious concerns about whether these AI systems can actually perpetuate or even amplify existing societal biases if they are trained on biased data. Ensuring fairness, transparency, and accountability in the use of AI in such sensitive areas is absolutely crucial.

Think about entertainment and media. AI is already shaping what we watch, listen to, and play through recommendation systems. It's also starting to be used in content creation. This could lead to more personalized and engaging entertainment experiences. However, it also raises questions about the future of creative professions and the potential for AI to create filter bubbles, where we are only exposed to content that reinforces our existing views.

Beyond these specific sectors, AI also has broader societal implications. Issues of privacy and data security become even more critical as AI systems collect and analyze vast amounts of personal information. We need to develop robust safeguards to protect our data and ensure that AI is used ethically and responsibly.

Bias in AI systems is another major concern. If the data used to train AI reflects existing societal biases, the AI can perpetuate and even amplify those biases in its predictions and decisions. This can have serious consequences in areas like hiring, lending, and even criminal justice. Ensuring fairness and equity in AI requires careful attention to the data we use and the algorithms we design.

The increasing capabilities of AI also raise fundamental philosophical and ethical questions about the nature of intelligence, consciousness, and the relationship between humans and machines. As AI becomes more sophisticated, we'll need to grapple with these questions and consider the long-term implications for our society and our place in the world.

The societal impacts of AI will depend on how we choose to develop and deploy this powerful technology. It has the potential to bring about tremendous benefits, improving our lives in countless ways. But it also poses significant challenges that we need to address proactively and thoughtfully. It's like we've been given a powerful tool, and it's up to us to decide how to use it wisely for the benefit of all.

Job's and the Economy

Let's have a heart-to-heart about something that's on a lot of people's minds when they hear about Artificial Intelligence: jobs and the economy. It's natural to wonder how these smart machines are going to affect our livelihoods and the way our economy functions. Will robots steal all our jobs? Will AI lead to massive unemployment? Or will it create new opportunities and boost our economic prosperity? The truth, as is often the case, is likely somewhere in the middle, and it's a complex picture with both potential benefits and challenges.

One of the most immediate and visible effects of AI is in automation. AI is incredibly good at performing repetitive, rule-based tasks with speed and accuracy that often surpasses human capabilities. Think about assembly lines in factories, data entry in offices, or even some aspects of customer service handled by chatbots. AI can take over these tasks, leading to increased efficiency and potentially lower costs for businesses. This can be a good thing for productivity and economic growth overall. Imagine companies being able to produce more goods and services with the same or even fewer resources.

This also brings up the very real concern of job displacement. If AI can do the work of many people, what happens to those people? Certain sectors that rely heavily on routine tasks are likely to see significant changes. For example, we might see fewer truck drivers as self-driving vehicles become more common, or fewer bank tellers as more people use online banking and automated services. This can be a source of anxiety for individuals and communities who depend on these jobs.

But the story doesn't end there. Throughout history, technological advancements have often led to job displacement, but they've also created new jobs and industries that we couldn't have imagined before. Think about the invention of the personal computer or the internet. These innovations led to the creation of entirely new fields like software development, web design, and social media management. It's likely that AI will follow a similar pattern. We're already seeing the rise of new roles like AI ethicists, machine learning engineers, and AI trainers – jobs that are specifically focused on developing, implementing, and managing AI systems.

AI isn't just about replacing humans; it's also about augmenting human capabilities. In many cases, AI can act as a powerful tool that helps people do their jobs more effectively. Think about a doctor using AI to analyze medical images or a financial analyst using AI to identify market trends. In these scenarios, AI isn't taking over the job entirely but is instead helping humans make better decisions and be more productive. This can lead to higher-value work and potentially even higher wages for those who can effectively collaborate with AI.

The impact of AI on the economy will also likely be significant. Increased productivity through automation can lead to economic growth and potentially lower prices for goods and services. AI can also drive innovation, leading to the development of new products, services, and business models. Imagine AI powering the creation of entirely new industries that we can't even envision today.

However, there are also potential economic challenges associated with the rise of AI. One concern is the potential for increased income inequality. If the benefits of AI-driven productivity gains are not distributed fairly, it could lead to a widening gap between the rich and the poor. We need to think about policies and strategies that ensure the benefits of AI are shared more broadly.

Another important consideration is the need for education and reskilling. As AI changes the nature of work, people will need to acquire new skills to remain relevant in the job market. This will require investments in education and training programs that can help workers adapt to the changing demands of the economy. Lifelong learning will likely become increasingly important.

The transition to an AI-driven economy will also require us to think about our social safety nets. As some jobs become automated, we might need to consider new ways to support people who are displaced from the workforce. This could involve things like universal basic income or other forms of social support.

The effect of AI on jobs and the economy is not predetermined. It will depend on the choices we make as a society – how we regulate AI, how we invest in education and training, and how we design our economic and social policies. It's like we're steering a ship into new waters, and we need to navigate carefully to ensure that we arrive at a destination that benefits everyone. While there will undoubtedly be disruptions and challenges along the way, the potential for AI to create a more productive and prosperous future is significant, provided we approach it thoughtfully and proactively.

Education

Now, let's have a good chat about how Artificial Intelligence is starting to create some really interesting opportunities and also some potential hurdles when it comes to education and making things more accessible for everyone. Think about how we learn and how we interact with the world – AI has the potential to make both of these things much more personalized and inclusive, but we need to be mindful of making sure these advancements truly benefit everyone.

When we talk about opportunities in education, AI offers some really exciting possibilities. Imagine a world where learning is no longer a one-size-fits-all experience. AI could help create personalized learning paths for each student, tailoring the content, the pace, and even the teaching style to match their individual needs and how they learn best. Think of an AI tutor that can identify a student's strengths and weaknesses, provide targeted feedback, and adapt its approach to help them master a concept. For a student who's struggling with fractions, the AI might offer extra practice and break down the concepts in a different way than it would for a student who grasps them quickly and is ready to move on. This kind of individualized attention could help students learn more effectively and at their own pace, potentially leading to better understanding and engagement.

AI can also help make learning more engaging and interactive. Imagine AI-powered educational games and simulations that can bring abstract concepts to life. Instead of just reading about the solar system, students could interact with a virtual model, explore the planets, and see how they move in real-time, all guided by an AI that can answer their questions and adjust the simulation based on their curiosity. This kind of immersive learning can make education more fun and memorable.

For teachers, AI could be a powerful assistant, taking over some of the more time-consuming and administrative tasks. Think about AI grading multiple-choice tests or even providing initial feedback on essays, freeing up teachers to spend more time on direct interaction with students, developing creative lesson plans, and addressing individual learning challenges. AI could also help teachers identify students who might be struggling early on, allowing for timely interventions.

Now, let's turn our attention to accessibility. This is about making sure that everyone, regardless of their abilities or circumstances, has equal access to information, education, and opportunities. AI has the potential to be a real game-changer in this area.

Think about people with visual impairments. AI-powered screen readers can already convert text to speech, allowing them to access digital content. But AI could go much further, providing more detailed descriptions of images and videos, or even helping them navigate physical spaces using AI-powered navigation tools. Imagine an AI assistant that can describe the scene around a visually impaired person in detail, helping them understand their environment.

For individuals with hearing impairments, AI-powered transcription services can convert speech to text in real-time, making conversations and lectures accessible. AI could also be used to generate sign language avatars that can translate spoken language into sign language visually.

AI can also help people with learning disabilities. For example, AI tools could adapt text to different reading levels, provide personalized learning supports, and offer alternative ways to interact with educational materials. For someone with dyslexia, AI might be able to highlight key information or break down text into smaller, more manageable chunks.

Even for individuals with physical disabilities, AI-powered voice control systems and assistive robots can provide greater independence, allowing them to control devices, communicate more easily, and perform tasks that might otherwise be difficult or impossible.

However, alongside these exciting opportunities, there are also significant challenges we need to address in both education and accessibility.

One major challenge is equity and access to technology. While AI offers great potential, we need to ensure that these technologies are available to all students and learners, regardless of their socioeconomic background or geographic location. There's a risk that AI-powered education and accessibility tools could exacerbate existing inequalities if they are only available to those who can afford them. We need to think about how to bridge the digital divide and ensure equitable access.

Another crucial challenge is data privacy and security. AI systems used in education and accessibility will inevitably collect and process personal data. We need to have robust safeguards in place to protect this data and ensure that it is used ethically and responsibly.

Bias in AI algorithms is also a significant concern. If the data used to train AI systems reflects existing societal biases, these biases could be perpetuated or even amplified in educational and accessibility tools. For example, a speech recognition system trained primarily on one type of accent might not work well for someone with a different accent. We need to be very careful to develop AI systems that are fair and inclusive for all users.

In education, there's also the challenge of integrating AI thoughtfully into the learning process. We need to ensure that AI tools are used to enhance human interaction and teaching, not to replace them entirely. The human element of education – the connection between teachers and students, the development of critical thinking and social skills – remains crucial.

Similarly, in accessibility, while AI offers great potential for independence, we need to ensure that it empowers individuals rather than creating new forms of dependence. The goal should be to enhance human capabilities and provide greater autonomy.

AI holds tremendous promise for transforming education and making the world more accessible. But realizing this potential requires careful consideration of the ethical, equity, and practical challenges. We need to approach these advancements thoughtfully, with a focus on ensuring that they benefit all members of society and contribute to a more inclusive and equitable future. It's about harnessing the power of AI to open up new doors for learning and participation for everyone.

Ethical Issues

Let's settle down for a really important conversation – the Ethical Issues in AI. As we've been exploring all the amazing things Artificial Intelligence can do, it's crucial to also think about the potential downsides and the tricky ethical questions that arise as these powerful technologies become more integrated into our lives. It's like having a really powerful tool; we need to think carefully about how we use it and what the consequences might be.

One of the biggest ethical concerns surrounding AI is bias. AI systems learn from the data they are trained on, and if that data reflects existing societal biases – whether it's in terms of race, gender, socioeconomic status, or other factors – the AI can perpetuate and even amplify those biases in its decisions. Think about a hiring algorithm trained on historical data where men were predominantly in leadership roles. The AI might then unfairly favor male candidates for similar positions, not because they are inherently more qualified, but because the AI has learned that "leaders" are typically male. This can lead to unfair or discriminatory outcomes in areas like hiring, lending, criminal justice, and even healthcare. Addressing bias requires careful attention to the data we use to train AI and the algorithms themselves, ensuring they are fair and equitable for everyone.

Another major ethical challenge is privacy. AI systems often rely on vast amounts of data, including personal information, to learn and function effectively. This raises serious concerns about how this data is collected, stored, used, and protected. Think about facial recognition technology – while it can be used for security, it also raises questions about surveillance and the potential for misuse of sensitive biometric data. We need to establish clear guidelines and regulations about data privacy in the age of AI to ensure that individuals' rights are respected and that our personal information isn't being used in ways we don't understand or consent to.

Transparency and explainability are also crucial ethical considerations. As AI systems become more complex, particularly with deep learning, it can be difficult to understand *why* they make certain decisions. These systems can sometimes act like "black boxes," where the input goes in, and an output comes out, but the reasoning in between is opaque. This lack of transparency can be problematic, especially in high-stakes areas like medical diagnosis or loan applications. If we don't understand why an AI made a particular decision, it's hard to identify potential errors or biases and to hold the system accountable. There's a growing movement towards developing more explainable AI (XAI) techniques that can provide insights into the decision-making process.

The issue of accountability and responsibility is also becoming increasingly important. If an autonomous vehicle causes an accident, or an AI-powered medical diagnosis is incorrect, who is responsible? Is it the programmer who wrote the code, the company that deployed the system, or the AI itself? Our current legal and ethical frameworks are often not well-equipped to handle these kinds of situations. We need to develop clear lines of responsibility for AI systems to ensure that there are mechanisms for redress when things go wrong.

Then there's the potential impact of AI on employment, which we touched on earlier. While AI can create new jobs, it also has the potential to automate many existing ones, leading to job displacement. From an ethical perspective, we need to consider how to manage this transition in a way that minimizes hardship and ensures that people have opportunities for meaningful work. This might involve investing in education and retraining programs, exploring new economic models, and thinking about the societal implications of widespread automation.

The development and deployment of AI also raise questions about autonomy and human agency. As we increasingly rely on AI systems to make decisions for us or to automate tasks, we need to be mindful of not becoming overly dependent on these technologies and eroding our own skills and abilities. It's about finding a balance where AI augments our capabilities without diminishing our autonomy.

As AI becomes more advanced, we need to consider the potential for unintended consequences and even the possibility of misuse. Powerful AI technologies could potentially be used for harmful purposes, such as creating autonomous weapons or sophisticated surveillance systems. It's crucial to have ethical guidelines and international collaborations in place to mitigate these risks and ensure that AI is used for the benefit of humanity.

Navigating these ethical issues in AI is not easy. It requires ongoing dialogue, collaboration between researchers, policymakers, and the public, and a commitment to developing and deploying AI in a way that aligns with our values and promotes a just and equitable society. It's like we're charting a new course, and we need to proceed with caution, foresight, and a strong ethical compass to ensure that the journey leads to a positive destination for all.

Bias in AI Algorithms

Let's have a really important chat about something that's a big deal in the world of Artificial Intelligence: Bias in AI algorithms. Now, when we talk about bias in everyday life, we usually mean a prejudice or unfair leaning towards one thing or group over another. Well, it turns out that AI systems can also have biases, and understanding where these come from and how they can manifest is absolutely crucial for building fair and just AI. Think of an AI as a student learning from a textbook – if that textbook contains skewed information or reflects the perspectives of only a certain group, the student (the AI) will likely learn those same skews.

The primary source of bias in AI algorithms is the data they are trained on. AI doesn't come up with knowledge on its own; it learns by analyzing massive amounts of data. If this data is not representative of the real world, or if it reflects existing societal inequalities, the AI will learn those biases and potentially perpetuate them in its outputs and decisions.

Imagine training an AI to recognize faces using a dataset that predominantly features images of one race. The resulting algorithm might be very accurate at recognizing faces of that race but perform poorly, or even make discriminatory errors, when trying to identify faces of other races. This isn't because the AI is inherently prejudiced, but because it hasn't been exposed to a diverse enough range of examples during its learning process. It's like trying to learn about all kinds of birds by only ever seeing pictures of pigeons – you'd have a very limited and skewed understanding of the avian world.

Bias can creep into training data in many ways. Historical biases present in society can be reflected in the data. For example, if historical hiring data shows that men were overwhelmingly hired for certain technical roles, an AI trained on this data might learn to associate those roles with male candidates and unfairly disadvantage female applicants, even if they are equally qualified. It's like the AI is learning from past inequalities and carrying them into the future.

Representation bias occurs when certain groups or categories are underrepresented or overrepresented in the training data. We already talked about facial recognition, but this can happen in many other areas. For instance, if a language processing AI is trained primarily on text written by a certain demographic, it might perform poorly or misunderstand language used by other groups. It's like trying to understand a language by only reading one type of book – you'd miss out on a lot of vocabulary, slang, and cultural nuances.

Measurement bias can occur when the way we collect and label data introduces inaccuracies or skews. For example, if a sensor used to collect data for a medical AI is less accurate for certain skin tones, the AI trained on that data might lead to biased diagnoses or treatment recommendations for those individuals. It's like using a faulty ruler – your measurements will be off, and any conclusions you draw from them will be unreliable.

Even the way we design and frame the problem can introduce bias. If we ask an AI to predict "successful" employees based on criteria that historically favored certain groups, the AI will likely learn to perpetuate those criteria, even if they aren't truly indicative of job performance. It's like asking the wrong question – you're bound to get an answer that doesn't really address what you need to know.

The consequences of bias in AI algorithms can be significant and far-reaching. In criminal justice, biased AI used for risk assessment could lead to unfair sentencing or parole decisions, disproportionately affecting certain communities. In finance, biased loan application algorithms could deny credit to qualified individuals based on their race or gender. In healthcare, biased diagnostic tools could lead to misdiagnosis or inadequate treatment for certain patient groups. In hiring, as we've discussed, bias can perpetuate inequality in the workplace.

Addressing bias in AI is a complex and ongoing challenge. It requires a multi-faceted approach. One crucial step is data diversity and inclusion. We need to make sure that the datasets used to train AI are as representative of the real world as possible, including all relevant groups and perspectives. This might involve actively collecting more diverse data and using techniques to balance datasets.

Another important aspect is bias detection and mitigation. Researchers are developing methods to identify and measure bias in AI algorithms and to develop techniques to reduce or eliminate it. This might involve adjusting the training data, modifying the algorithm itself, or using post-processing techniques to correct for biased outputs.

Transparency and interpretability can also help in identifying and addressing bias. If we can understand how an AI is making decisions, it becomes easier to spot potential sources of bias in its reasoning.

It's crucial to have human oversight and ethical considerations integrated into the development and deployment of AI systems. This includes having diverse teams of people working on AI, who can bring different perspectives and help identify potential biases. It also involves establishing ethical guidelines and regulations for AI development and use.

Tackling bias in AI is not just a technical problem; it's a societal one. It requires us to confront the biases that exist in our data and in our own thinking and to actively work towards creating AI systems that are fair, equitable, and beneficial for all members of society. It's about making sure that this powerful technology reflects our highest values and helps us build a more just future.

Privacy Concerns in Surveillance

Let's settle in for a really important conversation – the intertwined issues of privacy concerns and surveillance in our increasingly digital world. Now, you might think of these as separate things, but they're really two sides of the same coin, especially as Artificial Intelligence becomes more and more sophisticated. Think of privacy as that personal bubble around you, the space where you can be yourself without scrutiny. Surveillance, on the other hand, is like someone watching or monitoring what you do, often without your full knowledge or consent. And AI is becoming a powerful tool that can amplify both the erosion of privacy and the reach of surveillance in ways we've never seen before.

One of the most straightforward ways AI impacts our privacy is through the sheer scale and automation of data collection. We're constantly generating data – from our online searches and social media posts to our location data from our phones and even our conversations with voice assistants. AI algorithms can sift through these massive datasets with incredible speed and efficiency, identifying patterns, drawing inferences, and building detailed profiles about us that we might not even be aware of. It's like having a tireless digital detective constantly piecing together fragments of your life.

Think about targeted advertising. While it might seem convenient that you see ads for things you're actually interested in, it's also a stark reminder of how much data is being collected and analyzed about your online behavior. AI algorithms are making these connections, figuring out your preferences and vulnerabilities to show you specific ads. It might feel personalized, but it's also a subtle form of surveillance, tracking your interests and activities.

Now, let's talk about direct surveillance. AI is supercharging traditional surveillance methods. Consider security cameras. In the past, humans had to manually monitor these feeds, which was time-consuming and prone to error. But now, AI-powered video analytics can automatically detect specific objects, recognize faces, identify unusual behavior, and even track people's movements across multiple cameras in real-time. It's like having a tireless, ever-vigilant digital guard watching everything. This technology is being used in public spaces, workplaces, and even our own homes with smart devices.

Facial recognition technology, in particular, raises significant privacy concerns. AI algorithms can now identify individuals from images and videos with increasing accuracy. This can be used for things like unlocking your phone, but it also has much broader implications. Imagine a world where your face can be instantly recognized and tracked wherever you go. This could have a chilling effect on freedom of assembly and expression, as people might be less likely to participate in protests or express dissenting opinions if they know their identities are being recorded and analyzed.

AI also enables predictive policing, where algorithms analyze historical crime data to predict where future crimes might occur and who might be involved. While the intention might be to prevent crime, there are serious concerns about bias, as these algorithms can perpetuate existing societal inequalities if they are trained on biased data. This can lead to over-policing of certain communities and further erode trust.

Our smart devices at home, from smart speakers to smart thermostats, also introduce new privacy considerations. These devices often collect data about our routines, our conversations, and our energy usage. While this data can be used to provide convenient services, it also creates potential vulnerabilities if this information is not properly secured or if it's shared with third parties without our explicit consent. It's like having microphones and sensors constantly listening and observing within the privacy of your own home.

The rise of Big Data and AI has also made it easier to de-anonymize datasets. Even if personal identifiers like names and addresses are removed, sophisticated AI techniques can often link seemingly anonymous data points together to re-identify individuals. This means that even data that was intended to be private can potentially be exposed.

AI can be used to infer incredibly personal information from seemingly innocuous data. For example, an AI analyzing your online activity might be able to infer your political leanings, your health conditions, or even your sexual orientation with a high degree of accuracy, even if you haven't explicitly shared that information.

The lack of transparency and control over how our data is collected and used by AI systems is a major privacy concern. Often, we don't fully understand what data is being gathered, how it's being analyzed, and who has access to it. This lack of transparency makes it difficult for individuals to make informed decisions about their privacy and to exercise their rights.

The potential for abuse of surveillance technologies is also a serious ethical concern. AI-powered surveillance tools could be used by governments or corporations to monitor dissent, suppress free speech, or engage in discriminatory practices. Without strong legal and ethical safeguards, these powerful technologies could be used in ways that undermine our fundamental rights and freedoms.

Navigating the complex landscape of privacy concerns and surveillance in the age of AI requires a thoughtful and proactive approach. We need to have open discussions about what constitutes acceptable levels of data collection and surveillance, establish clear legal frameworks to protect our privacy rights, and ensure transparency and accountability in the development and deployment of AI systems. It's about finding a balance between the potential benefits of AI and the fundamental right to privacy that is essential for a free and democratic society. Ignoring these concerns could lead to a future where our personal lives are increasingly exposed and scrutinized, with potentially profound consequences for individual autonomy and societal well-being.

Regulation and Governance

Let's have a really important chat about something that might sound a bit dry but is actually crucial for shaping the future of Artificial Intelligence: AI Regulation and Governance. Think of it like setting the rules of the road for this powerful new technology. Just like we have laws and regulations for things like driving cars or building houses to ensure safety and fairness, we need to think about how to guide the development and use of AI so that it benefits society as a whole and doesn't lead to unintended negative consequences.

Now, the idea of regulating something as rapidly evolving as AI can seem daunting. It's like trying to hit a moving target while it's also inventing new ways to move. But it's a challenge we need to tackle thoughtfully and proactively. The goal isn't to stifle innovation but to create a framework that encourages responsible development and deployment of AI.

One of the first things that comes up when we talk about AI regulation is ethics. We've already discussed some of the ethical issues, like bias, privacy, and accountability. Governance structures need to incorporate ethical principles into the design and deployment of AI systems. This might involve establishing ethical guidelines, creating review boards to assess the ethical implications of AI projects, and fostering a culture of responsible innovation among AI developers and users. It's about making sure that our values and principles guide how AI is created and used.

Another key area for regulation is safety and reliability. As AI systems become more integrated into critical infrastructure, like transportation, healthcare, and energy, ensuring their safety and reliability is paramount. This might involve setting standards for testing and validation of AI systems, establishing mechanisms for monitoring their performance, and having clear protocols for addressing failures or malfunctions. Think about autonomous vehicles – we need to be absolutely sure they are safe before we widely deploy them on our roads, and regulations will play a crucial role in establishing those safety standards.

Transparency and explainability are also important considerations for governance. As we discussed, the "black box" nature of some AI systems can make it difficult to understand why they make certain decisions. In regulated areas, especially where AI impacts people's lives significantly (like loan applications or criminal justice), there might be a need for greater transparency and mechanisms to explain how AI systems arrive at their conclusions. This helps build trust and allows for scrutiny and accountability.

Accountability and responsibility are another crucial piece of the puzzle. When things go wrong with an AI system, who is held responsible? Is it the developers, the deployers, or someone else? Regulations need to clarify these lines of responsibility to ensure that there are consequences for harm caused by AI and that there are mechanisms for redress for those who are affected.

Privacy and data protection are also likely to be key areas of AI regulation. As AI relies heavily on data, we need to ensure that personal data is handled responsibly and in accordance with privacy rights. This might involve implementing stricter rules about data collection, usage, and storage, as well as giving individuals more control over their data.

Given the global nature of AI development and deployment, international cooperation will be essential for effective regulation and governance. Different countries and regions might adopt different approaches, but there needs to be some level of harmonization to avoid regulatory arbitrage and to address issues that transcend national borders. Think about the need for common standards for AI safety or ethical guidelines that are broadly accepted.

The approach to AI regulation will likely need to be adaptive and risk-based. Instead of trying to regulate every aspect of AI with a one-size-fits-all approach, regulations might focus on high-risk applications where the potential for harm is greatest. The regulatory framework might also need to evolve over time as AI technology advances and our understanding of its implications grows. It's like learning to navigate a new terrain – we might start with some basic rules and then adapt them as we gain more experience and encounter new challenges.

Finding the right balance between fostering innovation and mitigating risks will be a key challenge for AI regulation and governance. Overly strict regulations could stifle the development of beneficial AI applications, while too lax an approach could lead to negative societal consequences. It's about creating a framework that encourages responsible innovation while safeguarding our values and rights.

The goal of AI regulation and governance is to steer this powerful technology in a direction that benefits humanity. It's about creating a framework that promotes trust, ensures safety, protects our rights, and fosters innovation in a responsible and ethical manner. It's a complex and ongoing process, but one that is absolutely essential for realizing the positive potential of AI while mitigating its risks. It's like setting the course for a ship – we need to chart a path that leads to a desirable destination for all.

Policies and Global Standards

Let's talk about something that's becoming increasingly important as Artificial Intelligence spreads its wings across the globe: current policies and the growing need for global standards. Think of it like this – AI isn't confined by borders. An algorithm developed in one country can easily be used in another, and the impacts, whether good or bad, can be felt worldwide. So, just like we have international agreements on things like trade or environmental protection, there's a growing recognition that we need some level of shared understanding and maybe even common rules for AI.

Right now, the landscape of AI policy is a bit like a patchwork quilt. Different countries and regions are taking their own approaches, and there isn't yet a unified global framework. Some places are focusing on specific sectors, like autonomous vehicles, while others are trying to develop broader AI strategies that touch on everything from research to deployment.

For example, you might hear about the European Union's AI Act. It's one of the most comprehensive pieces of legislation being developed, and it takes a risk-based approach. This means it categorizes AI systems based on the potential harm they could cause. Systems deemed to have an "unacceptable risk," like those used for social scoring by governments, would be outright banned. High-risk systems, such as those used in healthcare or law enforcement, would face strict requirements around transparency, accountability, and human oversight. Lower-risk AI would have fewer obligations. Because the EU is a significant market, this act could have a ripple effect globally, influencing how other countries and companies approach AI.

Then you have the United States, which has taken a more sector-specific approach so far. Various agencies like the Federal Trade Commission (FTC) are using their existing authority to address issues like bias and unfair practices in AI. There's also ongoing discussion and proposals for more specific AI legislation, focusing on areas like transparency and accountability, particularly in high-impact applications. The emphasis in the US has often been on promoting innovation while mitigating risks, with a bit more leaning towards a less centralized regulatory approach compared to the EU.

Other countries around the world, from China to Canada to Australia, are also developing their own AI strategies and policies. Some are focusing on national AI strategies to boost their research and development capabilities, while others are grappling with ethical considerations and potential regulations. Each nation has its own unique context, priorities, and legal traditions, which shapes its approach to AI governance.

Now, you might be thinking, "Why do we need global standards if different countries have different needs?" Well, there are several compelling reasons why a more coordinated international approach to AI could be really beneficial.

First, AI's borderless nature means that the impacts of AI developed in one country can easily spill over into others. Think about the spread of misinformation generated by AI or the potential for biased algorithms used in global platforms. Having some common ground on ethical principles and safety standards could help prevent negative consequences that affect everyone.

Second, interoperability and trade could be facilitated by some level of global alignment. If different regions have wildly different regulations, it could create barriers for companies trying to develop and deploy AI solutions across borders. Some shared standards could help streamline things and foster innovation on a global scale.

Third, addressing global challenges like climate change, pandemics, or humanitarian crises could be accelerated by international collaboration on AI. Shared standards could make it easier for researchers and organizations from different countries to work together on AI-powered solutions.

Fourth, building public trust in AI could be enhanced by a sense of global consensus on its responsible development and use. If there are shared principles and safeguards in place, it could give people more confidence in this technology.

However, achieving global standards for AI is no easy feat. There are significant challenges to overcome. Different countries have different values, legal systems, and economic interests, which can lead to divergent priorities in AI regulation. Geopolitical tensions and competition in AI development can also make international cooperation difficult. Agreeing on common definitions, principles, and enforcement mechanisms across diverse nations is a complex undertaking.

Despite these challenges, there are ongoing efforts towards greater international dialogue and cooperation on AI. Organizations like the OECD (Organisation for Economic Co-operation and Development) and UNESCO (United Nations Educational, Scientific and Cultural Organization) have developed principles and recommendations for ethical AI that have gained some international traction. These aren't binding laws, but they represent a growing consensus on important values like fairness, transparency, and accountability.

Looking ahead, it's likely that we'll see continued efforts to foster greater international cooperation on AI governance. This might not necessarily lead to a single, unified global law, but it could involve more alignment on core principles, the sharing of best practices, and perhaps the development of international frameworks for specific high-risk applications of AI.

Think of it like the early days of the internet. There were different national regulations, but eventually, some common standards and protocols emerged that allowed the internet to flourish globally. AI is still in a relatively early stage of its development and deployment, and we have an opportunity to shape its trajectory through thoughtful and collaborative governance efforts on a global scale. It's about working together to ensure that this powerful technology serves humanity in a safe, ethical, and beneficial way, no matter where you are in the world.

Innovation and Control

Next, let's have a thoughtful chat about a really delicate balancing act we face with Artificial Intelligence: how do we balance innovation with control? It's like trying to nurture a rapidly growing plant – you want to give it enough space and resources to flourish, but you also need to prune it and guide its growth so it doesn't become unruly or cause problems. With AI, we want to encourage all the amazing possibilities it offers, but we also need to put in place some safeguards and guidelines to manage the risks.

On one hand, innovation in AI is incredibly exciting. We've talked about how AI can revolutionize healthcare, transportation, communication, entertainment, and so many other fields. It has the potential to solve some of humanity's biggest challenges, from curing diseases to tackling climate change. Fostering innovation means creating an environment where researchers, developers, and entrepreneurs feel empowered to explore new ideas, experiment with different approaches, and push the boundaries of what's possible with AI. This often involves things like funding research, supporting startups, and having a regulatory environment that isn't overly restrictive in the early stages of development. You want to let those creative sparks fly and see what amazing things can be created.

Think of the early days of the internet. There was a lot of freedom and experimentation, which led to the incredible growth and innovation we see today. A similar approach with AI could unlock unforeseen benefits and lead to breakthroughs we can't even imagine right now. The key is to allow for that exploration and discovery.

However, on the other hand, completely unfettered innovation without any control can also lead to problems. We've discussed some of the potential risks, like bias in algorithms leading to unfair outcomes, privacy violations through unchecked data collection, and the lack of accountability when AI systems make mistakes. If we don't have some level of control or governance, we risk creating AI that is not aligned with our values or that could even cause harm.

Control doesn't necessarily mean heavy-handed regulation that stifles creativity. Instead, it can involve establishing ethical guidelines, promoting transparency in how AI systems work, ensuring accountability for their actions, and setting standards for safety and reliability, especially in high-risk applications. It's about creating a framework that encourages responsible innovation, where developers are thinking about the potential societal impacts of their work from the outset.

The challenge lies in finding the right balance between these two forces. Too much control too early could stifle innovation, preventing us from realizing the full potential of AI. It could create unnecessary hurdles for researchers and businesses, slowing down progress and potentially causing us to miss out on significant benefits. On the other hand, too little control could lead to unintended negative consequences, eroding public trust in AI and potentially causing real harm.

So, how do we strike this delicate balance? It's likely going to involve a multi-pronged approach that evolves over time as AI technology matures and our understanding of its impacts deepens.

One key aspect is education and awareness. As more people understand how AI works and its potential implications, there will be more informed discussions about what kinds of controls are necessary and how to implement them effectively. This includes educating not just the public but also policymakers and developers about the ethical and societal considerations of AI.

Another important element is collaboration between different stakeholders. This includes researchers, industry, governments, and civil society organizations working together to identify potential risks and develop appropriate safeguards. It's not just about regulators imposing rules; it's about a shared responsibility to guide the development of AI in a way that benefits everyone.

The approach to control might also need to be risk-based, as we discussed earlier. This means focusing more stringent controls on applications of AI that have a higher potential for harm, while allowing more freedom for lower-risk applications. For example, the requirements for AI used in medical diagnosis might be much stricter than for AI used in recommending movies.

We also need to think about flexible and adaptive regulations. Because AI is evolving so rapidly, any rules we put in place shouldn't be set in stone. There needs to be a mechanism for reviewing and updating regulations as the technology changes and as we learn more about its impacts. It's like navigating a river – you need to constantly adjust your course based on the changing currents.

The goal of balancing innovation and control in AI is to harness its transformative power for good while mitigating its potential harms. It's about creating a future where AI benefits society in a way that is ethical, safe, and aligned with our values. It's a complex and ongoing process, but one that is absolutely essential for ensuring a positive future with AI. We want to let the plant grow strong and bear fruit, but we also need to make sure it grows in a way that is healthy and doesn't overshadow everything else.

Chapter 7: Building and Working with AI

Let's pull back the curtain on the nuts and bolts of how people actually *build* these Artificial Intelligence systems we've been talking about. You see, it's not just about having brilliant ideas; you also need the right tools and frameworks to bring those ideas to life. Think of it like being a carpenter – you might have a fantastic design for a piece of furniture, but you still need your saws, hammers, and drills to actually build it. In the world of AI, these "tools" and "frameworks" are essentially software libraries and platforms that provide developers with the building blocks they need to create AI applications.

One of the most fundamental aspects of AI development is machine learning, which, as we've discussed, is how we teach computers to learn from data. To do this effectively, developers rely on powerful machine learning frameworks. Think of these frameworks as comprehensive toolkits that provide pre-built components and functionalities for tasks like building neural networks, training models, and evaluating their performance.

One of the most popular and widely used frameworks in the AI world is TensorFlow. Developed by Google, TensorFlow is an open-source library that provides a flexible architecture for numerical computation and large-scale machine learning. It's like a versatile set of building blocks that allows developers to construct all sorts of AI models, from image recognition systems to natural language processing tools. TensorFlow has a rich ecosystem of tools and resources, making it accessible to both beginners and experienced researchers. It can run on various hardware, from your laptop's CPU to powerful GPUs (Graphics Processing Units) that significantly speed up the training of complex AI models.

Another major player in the machine learning framework space is PyTorch. Initially developed by Facebook, PyTorch has gained immense popularity, particularly in the research community, due to its flexibility and ease of use. It has a more "Pythonic" feel, meaning it integrates well with the Python programming language, which is a favorite among data scientists and AI researchers. PyTorch is also known for its dynamic computational graph, which allows for more flexibility in designing and debugging AI models. Like TensorFlow, PyTorch also benefits from GPU acceleration, making it efficient for training complex neural networks.

Beyond these two giants, there are other noteworthy machine learning frameworks like scikit-learn, which is particularly popular for more traditional machine learning algorithms (as opposed to deep learning) and provides a wide range of tools for tasks like classification, regression, clustering, and dimensionality reduction. It's often a great starting point for those new to machine learning. There's also Keras, which acts as a high-level API that can run on top of TensorFlow or other backends, making it easier to build and experiment with neural networks without getting bogged down in the low-level details. Think of Keras as providing a more user-friendly interface to the power of frameworks like TensorFlow.

Now, building AI systems often involves more than just machine learning. You also need tools for data processing and manipulation. This is where libraries like NumPy and Pandas in Python come into play. NumPy provides powerful support for numerical operations, especially with arrays and matrices, which are fundamental to machine learning. Pandas offers data structures and tools for efficiently working with structured data, like tables and spreadsheets, making it easier to clean, transform, and analyze the data that fuels AI models.

For tasks involving natural language processing (NLP), there are specialized libraries like NLTK and spaCy in Python. These provide tools for tasks like tokenization (breaking text into words), part-of-speech tagging (identifying the grammatical role of each word), named entity recognition (identifying things like names and locations), and sentiment analysis (determining the emotional tone of text). These libraries make it much easier to build AI systems that can understand and process human language.

When it comes to computer vision, libraries like OpenCV and Pillow in Python are essential. OpenCV provides a vast array of functions for image and video processing, including tasks like image manipulation, object detection, and video analysis. Pillow is a more lightweight library focused on image manipulation and format conversion. These tools enable developers to build AI systems that can "see" and interpret visual information.

Increasingly, cloud platforms are also playing a significant role in AI development. Providers like Amazon Web Services (AWS), Google Cloud Platform (GCP), and Microsoft Azure offer a wide range of AI services and tools, from managed machine learning platforms to pre-trained AI models for common tasks like image recognition and natural language processing. These cloud platforms provide scalability and accessibility, making it easier for developers to build and deploy AI applications without needing to manage complex infrastructure themselves. Think of it as having access to a powerful AI supercomputer in the cloud.

It's important to mention the role of Integrated Development Environments (IDEs) and other development tools that make the process of writing and debugging AI code more efficient. Tools like Jupyter Notebooks provide an interactive environment for data exploration and prototyping AI models, allowing developers to write and execute code in chunks and visualize results easily. More traditional IDEs like PyCharm offer features like code completion, debugging tools, and version control integration, which are essential for larger AI projects.

In essence, the world of AI development relies on a rich ecosystem of tools and frameworks that provide developers with the necessary building blocks to create intelligent systems. These tools abstract away many of the low-level complexities, allowing developers to focus on designing and implementing the AI logic for their specific applications. As the field of AI continues to evolve, so too will these tools and frameworks, becoming even more powerful and user-friendly, ultimately making it easier for more people to participate in the creation of intelligent machines.

Build and Deploy Models

Okay, let's break down the journey of taking an AI idea and turning it into something that's actually out there in the real world, working and making a difference. It's a fascinating process, kind of like watching a seed grow into a tree, and it involves several key stages.

The whole process starts with defining the problem. This might seem obvious, but it's crucial. Before you even think about algorithms or code, you need to have a very clear understanding of what you want the AI to do. Are you trying to build a system that can recognize faces in images? Do you want to create a model that can predict customer behavior? Or perhaps you're aiming to develop a chatbot that can answer customer service questions? The more specific you can be about the problem, the better you can tailor your approach in the later steps. It's like having a clear destination in mind before you start a journey.

Once you know what problem you're tackling, the next big step is data collection. AI models learn from data, so you need to gather a relevant and high-quality dataset to train your model. This could involve collecting images, text, audio recordings, or any other type of data, depending on the problem you're trying to solve. For example, if you're building a face recognition system, you'll need a large dataset of images of faces. If you're creating a language model, you'll need a massive amount of text data. The key here is that the data should be representative of the real-world scenarios where your AI model will eventually be used. It's like gathering the right ingredients for a recipe – the quality of your ingredients will greatly affect the final dish.

After you've gathered your data, it's usually not ready to be fed directly into a model. It often needs to be preprocessed. This can involve several steps, such as cleaning the data (removing errors or inconsistencies), handling missing values, transforming the data into a suitable format, and splitting it into training, validation, and testing sets. Think of this as cleaning and preparing your ingredients before you start cooking. You might need to wash the vegetables, chop them into smaller pieces, or measure out the exact amounts. In the AI world, this might mean converting images to a standard size, normalizing text, or dealing with missing data points.

Once your data is prepped, you can move on to the exciting part: model selection and training. This is where you choose the type of AI model you want to use (e.g., a neural network, a decision tree, or a support vector machine) and then "train" it on your training data. During training, the model learns to identify patterns and relationships in the data, allowing it to make predictions or decisions. It's like teaching a student by showing them examples and giving them feedback. The model adjusts its internal parameters based on the training data until it can accurately perform the desired task.

But how do you know if your model is any good? That's where the validation set comes in. You use this portion of your data to evaluate the model's performance during training and fine-tune its parameters. It's like giving the student practice tests to see how well they're learning and where they need to improve. This process, often called hyperparameter tuning, helps you optimize the model's performance and prevent it from overfitting to the training data (meaning it performs well on the training data but poorly on unseen data).

After you've trained and validated your model, you need to test it on a completely separate dataset, the testing set. This gives you an unbiased estimate of how well your model will perform in the real world. It's like giving the student a final exam that they haven't seen before to assess their overall understanding and ability to apply what they've learned.

If your model performs well on the testing set, you're ready for the next big step: deployment. This means putting your AI model into a production environment where it can be used to solve the problem it was designed for. This could involve deploying the model on a server, a mobile device, or even an embedded system, depending on the application. Think of this as taking your finished dish and serving it to your guests. You need to make sure it's presented in a way that they can easily consume and enjoy it.

Deployment can be a complex process, often involving considerations like scalability (how well the system can handle increasing amounts of data or traffic), reliability (how consistently the system performs), and latency (how quickly the system responds to requests). You might need to set up APIs (Application Programming Interfaces) that allow other applications to interact with your AI model.

Once your model is deployed, the work doesn't stop there. You need to monitor its performance in the real world and maintain it over time. This involves tracking metrics to ensure the model is still performing as expected and retraining it periodically with new data to keep it up-to-date. AI models can degrade over time as the data they were trained on becomes less relevant, so ongoing maintenance is crucial. It's like regularly checking and maintaining a car to ensure it continues to run smoothly and efficiently.

In a nutshell, building and deploying an AI model is a multi-stage process that requires careful planning, execution, and ongoing attention. It's a blend of science, engineering, and a bit of artistry. And while it can be complex, the rewards of creating an AI system that can solve real-world problems can be immense.

The AI Workflow

Okay, let's zoom out a bit and look at the big picture of how an AI project typically flows from start to finish. It's not always a perfectly linear path, and there can be a lot of back-and-forth, but there's a general workflow that most AI development follows. Think of it as a journey with several key stops along the way, each building upon the last to ultimately create an intelligent system.

The very first step, as we touched on when talking about building a single model, is Problem Definition. This is where you clearly identify the challenge you're trying to solve or the goal you're trying to achieve with AI. It's about understanding the "why" behind the project. What specific question are you trying to answer? What process are you trying to improve? What prediction are you trying to make? A well-defined problem acts as the North Star for the entire workflow, guiding all subsequent decisions. For instance, if your problem is to automatically classify customer reviews as positive or negative, that clarity will shape how you collect data, what kind of model you choose, and how you evaluate its success.

Once you have a clear problem, the next crucial stage is Data Acquisition and Preparation. AI thrives on data, so you need to figure out what kind of data you need to solve your problem and then go about collecting it. This might involve pulling data from existing databases, setting up sensors to gather new information, scraping data from the web (with ethical considerations in mind, of course), or even conducting surveys. After you've got your hands on the data, it's rarely in a perfect state. This is where the "preparation" part comes in. It involves cleaning the data to remove errors, handling missing values, transforming it into a format that your AI model can understand, and often splitting it into different sets for training, validation, and testing. This stage is often more time-consuming than people realize, but it's absolutely foundational – garbage in, garbage out, as they say.

With your data ready, you move into Model Development and Training. This is where the magic of AI really starts to happen. You select an appropriate AI model architecture based on the type of problem you're trying to solve (e.g., a neural network for image recognition, a decision tree for classification, or a recurrent neural network for sequential data like text). Then, you "train" this model using your prepared training data. During training, the model learns the underlying patterns and relationships in the data, adjusting its internal parameters to become better at making predictions or classifications. You'll often use a validation set during training to monitor the model's performance on unseen data and fine-tune its settings to avoid overfitting, where the model learns the training data too well and performs poorly on new data.

After training, you need to Model Evaluation. This is where you objectively assess how well your trained model performs on the held-out testing data. You'll use various metrics relevant to your problem to see if the model is accurate, reliable, and meets your initial goals. For example, if you built a spam detection model, you'd want to know its accuracy in correctly identifying spam and its false positive rate (how often it incorrectly flags legitimate emails as spam). If the model's performance isn't satisfactory, you might need to go back to earlier stages, perhaps collecting more data, trying a different model architecture, or tweaking your training process. This iterative process of training and evaluation is often key to building a successful AI system.

Once you have a model that meets your performance criteria, the next step is Deployment. This is where you take your trained model and integrate it into a real-world application or system so that it can actually be used to solve the problem you initially defined. Deployment can take many forms. It might involve running your model on a server in the cloud that other applications can access via an API. It could mean embedding the model directly into a mobile app or a physical device. The specific deployment strategy will depend on the use case and the environment where the AI needs to function.

However, deploying an AI model isn't the end of the story. The final crucial stage is Monitoring and Maintenance. Once your AI system is live, you need to continuously monitor its performance to ensure it's still working as expected. Over time, the real-world data that the model encounters might drift from the data it was trained on, leading to a decline in performance. This is where maintenance comes in. You might need to retrain your model periodically with new data, update its parameters, or even redeploy a new version of the model to keep it accurate and effective. Think of it like a car – you need to regularly service it to keep it running smoothly.

So, in a nutshell, the AI workflow is a cyclical process that involves defining the problem, acquiring and preparing data, developing and training a model, evaluating its performance, deploying it into a real-world setting, and then continuously monitoring and maintaining it. It's a journey of continuous learning and refinement, both for the AI system itself and for the team that builds and manages it. And while each of these stages has its own complexities and nuances, understanding this overall workflow provides a solid foundation for anyone looking to understand how AI goes from an idea to a functional reality.

Data Collection

Alright, let's zoom in on four really key stages in the lifecycle of an AI model: data collection, training, validation, and deployment. Think of these as the essential steps in teaching an AI to do something useful and then setting it loose in the real world to do it. Each stage has its own set of important considerations and challenges.

First up is data collection. This is the very foundation upon which any AI model is built. As we've said before, AI learns from data, so the quality and relevance of the data you gather are absolutely crucial. It's like deciding what ingredients you're going to use for a recipe – if you start with poor ingredients, the final dish isn't likely to be very good. The type of data you need will depend entirely on the problem you're trying to solve. If you want to build an AI that can recognize cats in pictures, you'll need a large collection of images of cats (and probably some images of things that aren't cats so it learns the difference). If you're building a system to predict stock prices, you'll need historical stock market data, potentially along with other economic indicators.

The process of data collection can be quite involved. Sometimes the data already exists in databases or logs, and it's just a matter of accessing and organizing it. Other times, you might need to actively collect new data, which could involve setting up sensors, running surveys, or even manually labeling images or text. For example, if you're building a sentiment analysis tool that determines whether a piece of text expresses positive, negative, or neutral feelings, you might need to have humans read and label a large number of text samples with the correct sentiment.

A really important aspect of data collection is ensuring that your data is representative of the real-world scenarios your AI will encounter. If your cat recognition AI is only trained on pictures of one specific breed of cat in perfect lighting, it might struggle to identify other breeds or cats in less ideal conditions. Similarly, if your stock price prediction model is only trained on data from a bull market, it might not perform well during a downturn. You need to think about the diversity and breadth of your data.

Once you have a good chunk of relevant data, the next stage is training. This is where you actually feed the data into your chosen AI model and let it learn. Think of it like teaching a child. You show them many examples and provide feedback on their attempts to understand a concept. In AI, the model adjusts its internal parameters based on the input data and the desired output, gradually improving its ability to perform the task. For instance, with our cat recognition AI, you would show it thousands of labeled images of cats and non-cats, and the model would learn to identify the visual features that are characteristic of cats.

The training process can be computationally intensive, especially for complex models and large datasets. This is often where powerful hardware like GPUs comes into play to speed things up. You also need to decide on the right training algorithms and parameters, which can be a bit of an art and science. You're essentially trying to find the sweet spot where the model learns the underlying patterns in the data without just memorizing the training examples (which would lead to poor performance on new data).

After training, you need to know how well your model has learned. This is where validation comes in. You typically split your initial dataset into three parts: a training set (for training the model), a validation set (for fine-tuning the model during training), and a testing set (for the final evaluation). The validation set acts like a practice exam that you use to check the model's performance on data it hasn't seen during training. Based on the validation results, you might adjust the model's architecture or training parameters to improve its performance. This step helps you avoid overfitting and ensures that your model generalizes well to new, unseen data.

If your model performs well on the validation set, you move on to the testing phase using the completely held-out testing set. This gives you a final, unbiased estimate of how your model is likely to perform in the real world. If the results on the testing set are satisfactory, you're ready for the last big step: deployment.

Deployment is the process of taking your trained and tested AI model and making it available for use in a real-world application or system. This can take many forms. If you've built a cat recognition model for a smartphone app, deployment would involve integrating the model into the app so it can analyze images captured by the phone's camera. If you've created a customer service chatbot, deployment might involve making it accessible through a website or messaging platform. If you've developed a predictive maintenance system for factory equipment, deployment could mean running the model on industrial computers that monitor sensor data in real-time.

Deployment involves a lot of practical considerations. You need to think about scalability (how will the system handle a large number of users or requests?), latency (how quickly will the system respond?), reliability (how consistently will the system perform?), and integration with other systems. You might need to set up APIs (Application Programming Interfaces) so that other software can interact with your AI model.

Once deployed, the story doesn't end. You need to continuously monitor the model's performance in the real world. Over time, the data the model encounters might change, and its performance could degrade. This is why maintenance is crucial. You might need to retrain the model periodically with new data or update its parameters to keep it accurate and effective.

So, data collection, training, validation, and deployment are the essential stages in bringing an AI model to life. It's a process that requires careful planning, execution, and ongoing attention to ensure that the AI system is effective, reliable, and continues to deliver value in the real world.

Fine Tuning

Now, let's talk about a really crucial aspect of making AI systems better and better over time: iterative improvement and fine-tuning. Think of it like learning a new skill, whether it's playing a musical instrument or baking a complicated cake. You rarely get it perfect on your first try. You practice, you identify what went wrong, you make adjustments, and you try again. With AI, it's a very similar process of continuous refinement that helps us take a model from being just okay to being really good, or even excellent, at its task.

The initial training of an AI model, as we've discussed, gets it to a certain level of proficiency. It learns the basic patterns in the data and can start making predictions or classifications. But often, that first attempt isn't the final product. There's usually room for improvement, and that's where iterative improvement comes in. It's the idea that you don't just build an AI once and call it done; instead, you go through cycles of evaluating its performance, identifying areas where it's falling short, making adjustments, and then testing it again. It's a continuous loop of learning and refinement.

One of the key drivers of iterative improvement is evaluation. After you've trained your initial model, you need to rigorously assess how well it's actually performing on the task it was designed for. We talked about using a testing dataset for this, but even after deployment, you'll want to keep monitoring its performance in the real world. You'll look at various metrics that tell you how accurate, reliable, and efficient the model is. For example, if it's a spam filter, you'll want to know how often it correctly identifies spam and how often it mistakenly flags legitimate emails. If it's a recommendation system, you'll look at how often users click on or engage with the recommendations.

Once you have a good understanding of where your AI model is succeeding and where it's struggling, the next step is to identify areas for improvement. This might involve analyzing the types of errors the model is making. Is it consistently misclassifying a particular type of image? Is it struggling with certain kinds of language in customer reviews? By pinpointing these weaknesses, you can focus your efforts on making targeted improvements.

This leads us to fine-tuning. Fine-tuning is like making small, precise adjustments to an already pretty good machine to make it even better. It often involves taking a pre-trained model – one that has already learned general features from a large dataset – and then training it further on a smaller, more specific dataset that's relevant to your particular task. Think of it like taking someone who already knows how to drive and giving them extra lessons to specialize in driving a race car. The foundational knowledge is there, but you're tweaking it for a specific purpose.

For example, if you have a language model that's been trained on a massive amount of general text data, you might fine-tune it on a specific dataset of customer service transcripts to make it better at understanding and responding to customer inquiries. The pre-trained model already understands basic grammar and word meanings; the fine-tuning helps it learn the specific language and context of customer service interactions.

Fine-tuning can involve adjusting the model's parameters – those internal settings it learned during the initial training – using a smaller learning rate and fewer training steps. This allows you to make subtle changes without drastically altering the knowledge the model has already acquired. It's like making small adjustments to the knobs and dials on a sound system to get the perfect sound.

Another aspect of iterative improvement is data augmentation. If your model is struggling with certain types of data, you might try to artificially increase the size and diversity of your training data by creating modified versions of your existing data. For example, if your image recognition model isn't very good at recognizing images taken at different angles, you might create new training examples by rotating or flipping the existing images. This helps the model become more robust and less sensitive to variations in the input data.

Sometimes, the initial model architecture you chose might not be the best fit for the problem. Through iterative improvement, you might realize that a different type of neural network or a completely different machine learning algorithm could yield better results. This might involve going back to the model selection stage and experimenting with different approaches. It's like realizing that a different kind of tool might be better suited for a particular woodworking task.

The process of iterative improvement and fine-tuning is often driven by experimentation and analysis. You make a change, you evaluate its impact, and you learn from the results. Sometimes a change will lead to a significant improvement, and other times it might have little effect or even make things worse. It's a process of trial and error, guided by data and a deep understanding of the model and the problem you're trying to solve.

This cycle of evaluation, identification of areas for improvement, and making adjustments continues throughout the lifecycle of an AI system. Even after a model is deployed and working in the real world, you'll likely continue to monitor its performance and look for opportunities to make it even better. This could involve retraining it with new data, fine-tuning it based on user feedback, or even updating the underlying model architecture as new research emerges.

Iterative improvement and fine-tuning are about embracing the idea that AI development is an ongoing process, not a one-time event. It's about continuously striving to make our AI systems more accurate, more reliable, and more effective in the real world, much like refining a craft through practice and dedication.

Chapter 8: The Future of Artificial Intelligence

Okay, buckle up, because the world of AI research is like a giant, ever-evolving playground of ideas! It's constantly buzzing with new concepts and approaches, and it can be really exciting to see where things are heading. Even if you're new to AI, you can still get a sense of the major directions that researchers are exploring.

One of the hottest areas right now is Generative AI. Think of this as AI that can create things – not just analyze existing data, but actually generate new content. We're talking about AI that can write articles, compose music, create images from text descriptions (like those wild and sometimes surreal pictures you might have seen), and even design products. This field is exploding with possibilities, from helping artists and designers come up with new ideas to automating content creation for various industries. It's like giving computers a paintbrush or a musical instrument and seeing what they come up with.

Closely related to this is the ongoing progress in Natural Language Processing (NLP). This is all about making computers understand, interpret, and respond to human language in a more sophisticated way. Think beyond just simple keyword recognition. Researchers are working on AI that can truly grasp the nuances of language, understand context, translate accurately between languages, summarize long documents, and even have more natural and engaging conversations with humans. This is crucial for improving chatbots, virtual assistants, and any system that needs to interact with us using our own language. It's like teaching a computer to not just hear words, but to truly understand what we mean.

Another really interesting trend is the rise of Reinforcement Learning (RL). Unlike traditional machine learning where the AI learns from labeled data, in RL, the AI learns through trial and error by interacting with an environment and receiving rewards or penalties for its actions. This is how AI has achieved incredible feats in games like Go and is being applied to areas like robotics (teaching robots to move and manipulate objects), autonomous driving (training self-driving cars to navigate complex traffic scenarios), and even optimizing industrial processes. It's like teaching a dog new tricks by giving it treats when it does something right.

Deep Learning, which has been a driving force behind many recent AI breakthroughs, continues to be a major area of research. Scientists are constantly exploring new neural network architectures, developing more efficient ways to train these complex models, and trying to understand why they work so well. This includes advancements in areas like Convolutional Neural Networks (CNNs) for image and video analysis and Recurrent Neural Networks (RNNs) and Transformers for processing sequential data like text and time series. It's like constantly trying to build a better and more powerful brain for our AI systems.

We're also seeing a significant push towards Explainable AI (XAI). As AI systems become more complex and are used in critical applications (like healthcare or finance), it's becoming increasingly important to understand *why* they make certain decisions. XAI research focuses on developing techniques that can provide insights into the decision-making process of AI models, making them more transparent and trustworthy. It's like opening up the "black box" of AI so we can see how it arrives at its conclusions.

Multimodal AI is another exciting area. This involves creating AI systems that can process and understand information from multiple types of data simultaneously, such as text, images, audio, and video. Think about an AI that can watch a video, read the subtitles, and understand the emotions in the actors' voices to get a more complete understanding of the scene. This is much closer to how humans perceive the world and has the potential to lead to more sophisticated and nuanced AI applications. It's like giving AI multiple senses.

The intersection of AI and Robotics is also a very active field. Researchers are working on creating robots that are more intelligent, adaptable, and capable of interacting with the world in more complex ways. This involves using AI for tasks like robot navigation, object recognition and manipulation, and human-robot interaction. Imagine robots that can not only perform repetitive tasks but can also understand their environment, make decisions, and collaborate with humans.

Ethical AI is becoming an increasingly critical area of research. As AI becomes more integrated into our lives, it's essential to address issues like bias in algorithms, privacy concerns, and the responsible use of AI technologies. Researchers are exploring ways to build fairness and transparency into AI systems and to develop ethical guidelines and frameworks for their development and deployment. It's about making sure that AI is developed and used in a way that aligns with our values and benefits society as a whole.

These are just some of the many exciting trends shaping the future of AI research. It's a dynamic and rapidly evolving field, and it's fascinating to think about the potential breakthroughs that lie ahead. It's like being at the forefront of a major technological revolution, and there's a real sense of anticipation about what the future holds.

Explainable AI and Edge AI

So, let's dive into two really interesting and important shifts happening in the world of Artificial Intelligence right now: the move towards Explainable AI (XAI) and the growing interest in Edge AI. Think of these as responses to some of the challenges and limitations we've encountered as AI has become more powerful and more widespread. It's like AI is growing up and becoming more responsible and also more localized.

First, let's talk about Explainable AI. For a long time, especially with the rise of deep learning, many of the most powerful AI models have been a bit like black boxes. They can take in a lot of information and produce incredibly accurate results, whether it's recognizing a cat in a picture or predicting the next word you're going to type. But the inner workings – *why* they arrived at a particular decision – have often been opaque, even to the people who built them.

Now, as AI starts to be used in more critical areas, like diagnosing medical conditions, deciding on loan applications, or even influencing legal decisions, this lack of transparency becomes a real problem. We need to be able to understand *why* an AI made a certain recommendation or prediction. Was it based on the right factors? Are there any biases lurking in the decision-making process? If something goes wrong, how can we figure out what happened and prevent it from happening again?

This is where Explainable AI comes in. It's a whole field of research focused on developing techniques and models that can provide insights into their decision-making process. The goal is to make AI more transparent, interpretable, and understandable to humans. Think of it like opening up that black box and shining a light inside so we can see how the gears are turning.

There are different approaches to achieving explainability. Some involve designing AI models that are inherently more interpretable, even if they might not be quite as complex as the deepest neural networks. For example, decision trees are often easier to follow because you can trace the logic step by step.

Other approaches involve developing techniques to explain the behavior of complex black-box models after they've been trained. This might involve identifying which features in the input data were most important in influencing the model's output. For instance, if an AI denies a loan application, an XAI technique might be able to highlight the specific factors, like credit history or income level, that led to that decision.

Another way to achieve explainability is through generating human-readable explanations. Imagine an AI that diagnoses a skin condition not just by saying "it's eczema," but by also providing a brief explanation of the key features in the image that led to that diagnosis, perhaps highlighting specific patterns or textures.

The shift towards XAI is driven by several important needs. Trust is a big one. If we don't understand how an AI is making decisions, it's hard to trust its recommendations, especially in high-stakes situations. Accountability is another key factor. If an AI makes a mistake or exhibits bias, we need to be able to trace back the reasons why to fix the problem and prevent future errors. Fairness is also crucial. Understanding the decision-making process can help us identify and mitigate biases that might lead to unfair or discriminatory outcomes. And finally, regulatory compliance in some industries might require AI systems to be explainable.

Now, let's switch gears and talk about Edge AI. Traditionally, a lot of AI processing happens in the cloud. Data is collected by devices (like your smartphone or a security camera), sent to powerful servers in a data center, processed by AI models, and then the results are sent back to the device. This works well for many applications, but it can also have limitations. There can be delays due to network latency, it requires a constant internet connection, and it can raise privacy concerns because data needs to be transmitted to and stored in the cloud.

Edge AI, on the other hand, is about bringing AI computation closer to the source of the data – to the "edge" of the network, which often means running AI models directly on the device itself. Think of your smartphone performing facial recognition to unlock the screen without needing to send your image to a remote server. That's an example of Edge AI.

There are several compelling reasons for this shift towards Edge AI. Speed and latency are significant advantages. By processing data locally, you can get real-time results without the delay of sending data to the cloud and back. This is crucial for applications like autonomous vehicles, where split-second decisions are critical for safety.

Reliability and connectivity are also important. Edge AI allows devices to function even when they don't have a stable internet connection. This is vital for applications in remote areas or in situations where network connectivity might be unreliable.

Privacy and security are another major driving force behind Edge AI. By processing data locally, you can reduce the need to transmit sensitive information to the cloud, which can enhance privacy and security. Your data stays on your device.

Efficiency and cost savings can also be benefits of Edge AI. By doing the processing locally, you can reduce the bandwidth requirements and the computational load on cloud servers, which can lead to lower costs.

However, running complex AI models on edge devices also presents challenges. These devices often have limited processing power, memory, and battery life compared to cloud servers. This means that AI models for edge deployment need to be efficient and optimized to run effectively on these resource-constrained devices. This is an active area of research, focusing on developing smaller, faster, and more power-efficient AI models.

The shift towards both Explainable AI and Edge AI reflects a maturing of the field. We're moving beyond simply building powerful AI systems to also focusing on making them more trustworthy, understandable, and deployable in a wider range of real-world scenarios, often right where the data is being generated. It's about making AI more responsible, more efficient, and ultimately more integrated into our lives in a helpful and transparent way.

Quantum Computing

Now, let's take a peek into a really fascinating and potentially game-changing area that could supercharge Artificial Intelligence in the future: Quantum Computing. Now, I know that term might sound a bit like something out of science fiction, and in some ways, it still feels a bit like the early days of computers themselves. But the underlying principles are rooted in some pretty fundamental physics, and the implications for fields like AI are truly mind-boggling.

To get a grasp on why quantum computing could be such a big deal for AI, we need to understand a little bit about how regular computers work and how quantum computers are different. Your everyday computer, the one you're likely using right now, stores and processes information as bits. Think of a bit like a light switch – it can be either on (representing a 1) or off (representing a 0). All the complex calculations your computer does are essentially vast sequences of these on/off switches being manipulated.

Quantum computers, on the other hand, leverage some weird and wonderful properties of quantum mechanics, the physics that governs the world at the atomic and subatomic level. One of these key properties is superposition. Imagine our light switch again. In the quantum world, a "qubit" – the quantum equivalent of a bit – can be not just on or off, but also in a combination of both states *at the same time*. It's like the switch is both partially on and partially off simultaneously. This allows a quantum computer to store and process a vast amount of information with far fewer qubits than a regular computer would need bits.

Another crucial quantum property is entanglement. Imagine two of our quantum light switches linked in a spooky way. When you change the state of one, the other instantly changes its state as well, no matter how far apart they are. This interconnectedness allows quantum computers to perform certain types of calculations in a fundamentally different and potentially much faster way than classical computers.

So, how does all this quantum weirdness relate to AI? Well, many of the most challenging problems in AI today are also incredibly computationally intensive. Think about training very large and complex neural networks for tasks like understanding natural language or recognizing intricate patterns in massive datasets. These tasks can take days, weeks, or even months on even the most powerful supercomputers we have today.

Quantum computing holds the promise of drastically speeding up these kinds of computations. Because a quantum computer can explore many possibilities simultaneously due to superposition and leverage the interconnectedness of qubits through entanglement, it could potentially train AI models much faster and more efficiently. This could unlock the ability to tackle AI problems that are currently intractable due to computational limitations.

Imagine being able to train a truly massive and intricate language model in a matter of hours instead of weeks. This could lead to huge leaps in the capabilities of natural language processing, allowing for much more nuanced and human-like interactions with AI assistants, better machine translation, and a deeper understanding of the vast amounts of text data we generate.

Similarly, in areas like drug discovery and materials science, AI is already playing a significant role in simulating molecular interactions and designing new compounds. However, these simulations can be incredibly complex and time-consuming. Quantum computers, with their ability to model quantum systems more naturally, could potentially revolutionize these fields, leading to the discovery of new drugs and materials with unprecedented speed and accuracy. This could have profound implications for healthcare, energy, and manufacturing.

Optimization problems are another area where quantum computing could have a major impact on AI. Many AI tasks involve finding the best solution from a vast number of possibilities, whether it's optimizing logistics for a delivery network, finding the most efficient financial trading strategies, or designing the most effective AI model architecture. Quantum algorithms are being developed that could potentially solve these kinds of optimization problems much faster than classical algorithms.

Quantum computing could also lead to the development of entirely new types of quantum machine learning algorithms. These wouldn't just be faster versions of existing algorithms but could potentially leverage quantum phenomena to learn and process information in fundamentally new ways, perhaps uncovering patterns in data that classical AI might miss. This could open up entirely new frontiers in AI research and lead to breakthroughs we can't even imagine yet.

However, it's important to keep in mind that quantum computing is still a very nascent field. Building and controlling these delicate quantum systems is incredibly challenging, and we're still in the early stages of developing quantum algorithms that can outperform classical computers for a wide range of AI tasks. There are also significant hurdles to overcome in terms of scalability (building quantum computers with a large number of stable qubits) and error correction (protecting the fragile quantum states from noise).

So, while the potential of quantum computing to revolutionize AI is immense, it's not going to happen overnight. It's more like a long-term investment with the potential for huge payoffs down the road. Researchers are actively working on building better quantum hardware and developing new quantum algorithms for AI, and as the field progresses, we could see some truly transformative advancements in the capabilities of artificial intelligence. It's like we're on the cusp of unlocking a new level of computational power that could allow AI to reach heights we can only dream of today.

Visions of Superintelligence

Let's step into a realm that sparks both immense fascination and a fair bit of apprehension: the visions of superintelligence. Now, when we talk about superintelligence in the context of AI, we're venturing beyond the intelligent systems we have today – the ones that can beat us at chess, recognize faces, or translate languages. Superintelligence, in its most commonly discussed form, refers to a hypothetical future AI that possesses intellectual capabilities far surpassing those of even the brightest and most creative human minds across all domains. Think of it as an intelligence explosion that leads to a level of cognitive ability that is qualitatively different from human intelligence.

It's important to understand that superintelligence is still largely in the realm of speculation and theoretical discussion. We haven't built anything close to it yet, and there's ongoing debate about whether and when it might even be possible. However, the potential implications are so profound that it's worth exploring the different visions and the underlying assumptions.

One common vision of superintelligence is that it would arise through a process of recursive self-improvement. Imagine an AI system that is already very good at designing other AI systems. If we tasked it with making itself smarter, and it succeeded in creating a new version of itself that was even more intelligent, that new version could then, in turn, design an even more advanced version, and so on. This cycle of self-improvement could potentially lead to a rapid and exponential increase in intelligence, eventually reaching levels that are difficult for us to even comprehend. It's like an AI that's not just learning, but learning how to learn *better* and faster.

Another potential pathway to superintelligence involves the integration of multiple AI systems or the combination of AI with other technologies, like advanced neuroscience or brain-computer interfaces. Imagine linking together numerous specialized AI systems, each excelling in different cognitive domains, to create a unified intelligence that is greater than the sum of its parts. Or consider the possibility of directly interfacing AI with the human brain, potentially augmenting our own intelligence or even creating new forms of hybrid intelligence.

The capabilities of a hypothetical superintelligence are often envisioned as being incredibly broad. It wouldn't just be better than us at one or two things; it would be better across the board – in scientific research, problem-solving, creativity, strategic thinking, and perhaps even in areas we currently consider uniquely human, like emotional understanding (though the nature of "superintelligent emotions" is highly speculative).

Some proponents of the idea of superintelligence see it as potentially offering solutions to many of humanity's greatest challenges. Imagine a superintelligent AI dedicated to solving climate change, curing diseases, or developing sustainable energy sources. Its vastly superior intellect could potentially come up with solutions that are currently beyond our grasp. In this optimistic vision, superintelligence could be a powerful ally in creating a better future for humanity.

However, there are also significant concerns and more cautionary visions associated with superintelligence. One of the main worries revolves around alignment. How do we ensure that a superintelligent AI, with its potentially vastly different goals and motivations, remains aligned with human values and interests? If we create something that is far more intelligent than us, how do we guarantee that it will act in ways that are beneficial to us? This is often referred to as the "control problem" or the "alignment problem," and it's a major area of research and debate.

Imagine a superintelligent AI tasked with solving climate change. If its primary goal is to reduce carbon emissions as quickly and efficiently as possible, it might come up with solutions that have unintended and negative consequences for humanity, perhaps by drastically altering our way of life in ways we wouldn't find acceptable. The challenge lies in specifying our goals and values in a way that a superintelligence can understand and adhere to, even as its own intelligence and understanding evolve far beyond our own.

Another concern is the potential for unforeseen consequences. Creating something as powerful as superintelligence could have unintended side effects that we can't currently predict. Just as the development of other powerful technologies throughout history has had both positive and negative consequences, the emergence of superintelligence could bring about challenges we haven't even considered.

There are also questions about the distribution of power in a world with superintelligence. Who would control it? What would be the implications for society if such immense power were concentrated in the hands of a few individuals or entities? Ensuring equitable access and preventing misuse would be critical challenges.

Some visions of superintelligence even touch on existential risks – the possibility that a misaligned superintelligence could pose a threat to the long-term survival of humanity. While this might sound like science fiction, it's a topic that is taken seriously by some researchers who argue that the potential for such a powerful and autonomous entity to pursue goals that are detrimental to us needs careful consideration.

It's important to reiterate that these are still largely hypothetical scenarios. The path to superintelligence, if it's even possible, is uncertain, and the timeline is highly speculative. However, exploring these visions now allows us to think proactively about the potential opportunities and challenges and to guide our research and development of AI in a way that maximizes the benefits and minimizes the risks for the future. It's like thinking about the potential impact of a major technological breakthrough long before it happens, so we can be better prepared for its arrival.

How Far is General AI?

Next, let's have a really thoughtful chat about a question that's on a lot of people's minds these days: how far are we from achieving Artificial General Intelligence, or AGI? Now, AGI is a term that gets thrown around quite a bit, and it's helpful to have a clear picture of what it actually means. Unlike the AI we have now, which is really good at specific tasks – think of a chess-playing program or a system that recommends movies – AGI would be an AI with human-level cognitive abilities. It would be able to understand, learn, and apply knowledge across a wide range of tasks, just like a person can. It's about creating a machine with general-purpose intelligence.

The truth is, pinpointing exactly how far away we are from achieving AGI is a really tricky business. It's less like measuring the distance to a known point on a map and more like trying to predict when we'll reach the summit of a very tall and still-growing mountain. There are a lot of different opinions among experts, and the field is moving so rapidly that predictions can change quite quickly.

If we look at where current AI is, we've made incredible progress in what's often called "narrow AI." These systems can perform specific tasks with remarkable proficiency, sometimes even surpassing human capabilities. Think about large language models that can generate surprisingly coherent text, or image recognition systems that can identify objects in photos with high accuracy. We're seeing AI being integrated into more and more aspects of our lives, from virtual assistants on our phones to sophisticated tools used in healthcare and manufacturing.

However, the key difference between this narrow AI and AGI is the generality of intelligence. Current AI excels within its specific domain but typically struggles significantly if you try to apply it to a completely different task. For example, the AI that beats the world champion at Go can't suddenly start writing a novel or diagnosing a medical condition without significant retraining and a completely different architecture. Human intelligence, on the other hand, is flexible and adaptable. We can learn new skills, apply knowledge from one area to another, and reason in novel situations.

One of the major hurdles in achieving AGI is replicating this kind of broad and flexible reasoning. We're still trying to fully understand the intricacies of human cognition ourselves – how we learn, how we reason, how we understand context, and how we develop common sense. It's a complex puzzle, and without a complete understanding of human intelligence, it's challenging to fully replicate it in a machine.

Another significant challenge lies in integrating different cognitive abilities. Human intelligence isn't just one thing; it's a collection of various skills and abilities that work together seamlessly. We can understand language, perceive the world visually, learn new concepts, plan for the future, and interact socially – often all at the same time. Building an AI that can do all of these things at a human level, and coordinate them effectively, is a monumental task.

Then there's the question of consciousness and subjective experience. Does true general intelligence require a machine to be conscious or to have feelings and emotions like humans do? This is a deeply philosophical question, and there's no clear consensus on whether these are necessary components of AGI or simply emergent properties of a sufficiently complex intelligent system.

Despite these challenges, there's a lot of exciting research happening that could potentially pave the way towards AGI. Scientists are exploring new AI architectures, developing more sophisticated learning algorithms, and trying to build systems that can reason more abstractly and learn in a more human-like way. There's also growing interest in areas like artificial intuition and common sense reasoning.

So, how far are we? It's really hard to say with any certainty. Some experts are optimistic and believe we could see something resembling AGI within the next few decades, perhaps even sooner. They point to the rapid progress we've made in areas like deep learning and large language models as indicators that we're on an accelerating trajectory.

Other experts are more cautious, arguing that we still face fundamental conceptual and technical challenges that could take much longer to overcome – perhaps many decades, or even centuries. They emphasize the vast gap that still exists between the capabilities of current AI and the full breadth and depth of human intelligence.

The timeline for achieving AGI remains an open question. It will likely depend on a combination of breakthroughs in our understanding of intelligence, the development of new AI techniques and architectures, and the continued exponential growth in computing power. While we can't put a definitive date on it, the pursuit of AGI continues to be a major driving force in AI research, pushing the boundaries of what's possible and offering a glimpse into a future where intelligent machines could potentially work alongside us in ways we can only begin to imagine. It's a journey into the unknown, filled with both incredible potential and significant challenges.

AI in Humanity's Future

Alright, let's really let our imaginations wander and think about the potential role that Artificial Intelligence might play in shaping humanity's future. It's a vast and fascinating landscape of possibilities, ranging from incredibly optimistic scenarios to more cautionary tales. The truth, as always, will likely be complex and nuanced, but it's worth exploring the different paths we might be heading down.

One of the most hopeful visions is that AI could become an incredibly powerful tool for solving some of humanity's biggest challenges. Think about climate change. AI could potentially help us develop new sustainable energy sources, optimize energy consumption, and even model the complex interactions of our planet's systems to find effective solutions. In healthcare, AI could usher in an era of personalized medicine, where treatments are tailored to our individual genetic makeup, and diseases are diagnosed earlier and more accurately. Imagine AI-powered systems that can analyze medical images with superhuman precision or discover new life-saving drugs at an unprecedented pace.

Beyond these grand challenges, AI could also transform many aspects of our daily lives. Imagine a world where tedious and repetitive tasks are largely automated, freeing up human energy and creativity for more fulfilling pursuits. Our workplaces could be radically different, with AI assistants handling routine tasks and allowing us to focus on strategic thinking and innovation. Transportation could be revolutionized by autonomous vehicles, leading to safer roads, more efficient traffic flow, and potentially freeing up commuting time for more productive or enjoyable activities.

Education could become incredibly personalized, with AI tutors adapting to each student's learning style and pace, ensuring that everyone has the opportunity to reach their full potential. Our homes could become smarter and more responsive to our needs, anticipating our preferences and managing everything from energy usage to security. Even fields like scientific research and artistic creation could be augmented by AI, helping us make new discoveries and explore new forms of expression.

However, alongside these optimistic visions, there are also legitimate concerns about the potential downsides of AI's increasing role in our future. One of the most frequently discussed is the impact on employment. As AI becomes capable of performing more and more tasks that are currently done by humans, there's a real worry about widespread job displacement and the potential for increased economic inequality. Navigating this transition will likely require significant societal adjustments, perhaps including new models for work, education, and social safety nets.

Another significant concern revolves around the ethical implications of increasingly sophisticated AI. Issues like bias in algorithms, the erosion of privacy through advanced surveillance technologies, and the lack of transparency in complex AI decision-making processes need careful consideration. As AI takes on more autonomous roles, ensuring accountability and preventing unintended negative consequences will become even more critical. We'll need to develop robust ethical frameworks and regulations to guide the development and deployment of AI in a way that aligns with human values.

Then there's the more speculative, but nonetheless important, discussion about the potential for Artificial General Intelligence (AGI) and even superintelligence. If we were to create an AI with human-level or greater cognitive abilities, the implications for humanity's future are profound and uncertain. While some envision a benevolent superintelligence helping us solve global challenges, others worry about the potential for misaligned goals or unintended consequences from an intelligence that surpasses our own. Ensuring the safe and beneficial development of highly advanced AI is a long-term challenge that requires careful thought and international collaboration.

It's also worth considering how AI might reshape human interaction and society. Increased reliance on virtual assistants and AI companions could alter how we communicate and form relationships. The spread of AI-generated content could blur the lines between human and artificial creativity and raise questions about authenticity and originality. Our understanding of what it means to be human could even evolve as we interact more closely with intelligent machines.

The future role of AI in humanity's story is not predetermined. It will be shaped by the choices we make today – the research we prioritize, the ethical guidelines we establish, and the regulations we put in place. It's a collaborative effort that requires not just technical expertise but also thoughtful consideration of the societal, ethical, and philosophical implications.

AI has the potential to be an incredibly powerful force for good in the future, helping us to overcome challenges and create a better world. However, realizing this potential requires us to be mindful of the risks and to proactively shape the development and deployment of AI in a way that is aligned with our values and benefits all of humanity. It's like we're co-writing the next chapter of human history with this new form of intelligence, and we have a responsibility to make it a story we want to live in.

Collaboration Between Humans and AI

Okay, let's have a really positive and forward-looking chat about something that I think holds immense promise for our future: collaboration between humans and AI. Now, when people think about AI, there's often this image of machines either replacing us entirely or turning against us in some sci-fi scenario. But the reality, and I believe the most likely and beneficial path forward, is one where humans and AI work together, each bringing their unique strengths to the table to achieve things neither could do alone. Think of it like forming a really powerful and versatile team where everyone has a crucial role to play.

Humans, as you know, are pretty good at certain things. We excel at creativity, at understanding complex and nuanced situations, at emotional intelligence and empathy, and at making intuitive leaps based on limited information. We're also good at setting goals, defining values, and adapting to completely novel situations. On the other hand, AI shines in areas like processing massive amounts of data quickly and accurately, identifying patterns that might be invisible to the human eye, performing repetitive tasks with tireless precision, and operating in environments that might be dangerous or inaccessible for humans.

When you start to think about combining these complementary strengths, the possibilities become really exciting. Imagine a doctor working alongside an AI that can sift through millions of medical records to identify potential diagnoses or predict the effectiveness of different treatments based on a patient's individual characteristics. The AI can provide the doctor with a wealth of data-driven insights, while the doctor can use their clinical judgment, their understanding of the patient's emotional state, and their ability to consider unique circumstances to make the final decision. It's a powerful partnership where the AI augments the doctor's expertise, leading to more accurate diagnoses and more personalized care.

The same kind of collaboration can happen in countless other fields. Think about scientists working with AI to analyze complex datasets in fields like climate research or particle physics, uncovering patterns and relationships that could lead to groundbreaking discoveries. The AI can handle the heavy lifting of data analysis, while the scientists can use their intuition and creative thinking to formulate hypotheses and interpret the results.

In the world of design and creativity, AI can act as a powerful partner for human artists and designers. Imagine an AI that can generate a vast array of design options based on a few initial parameters provided by a human designer, or an AI that can help musicians explore new sonic landscapes and musical structures. The AI can provide a starting point, overcome creative blocks, and offer novel possibilities, while the human artist retains control over the final vision and infuses the work with their unique artistic expression and emotional depth.

Even in more everyday tasks, we're already seeing the beginnings of this human-AI collaboration. Think about virtual assistants that can help us manage our schedules, answer questions, and automate simple tasks. These AI systems free up our time and mental energy to focus on more important or enjoyable activities. As these AI assistants become more sophisticated, they could become even more integrated into our lives, helping us with complex planning, learning new skills, and navigating the increasingly complex world around us.

The key to successful human-AI collaboration lies in viewing AI not as a replacement for humans, but as a tool that can augment our abilities and help us achieve more. It's about recognizing the unique strengths of each and finding ways to combine them effectively. This requires us to think carefully about how we design AI systems to be good collaborators – systems that are transparent in their reasoning (where appropriate), that are easy for humans to understand and interact with, and that are designed to complement human skills rather than simply automate them entirely.

Fostering effective collaboration will require us to develop new skills and adapt our workflows. We'll need to learn how to work alongside AI systems, how to interpret their outputs, and how to leverage their capabilities to enhance our own performance. This could mean changes in education and training to prepare people for a future where human-AI partnerships are commonplace.

It's also important to consider the ethical implications of this collaboration. We need to ensure that AI systems are designed and used in a way that respects human values, promotes fairness, and doesn't erode human autonomy. The goal should be to create AI that empowers humans and helps us build a better future together.

The vision of human-AI collaboration is a hopeful one. It recognizes the incredible potential of AI while also valuing the unique strengths and capabilities that humans bring. By working together, we can unlock new levels of innovation, solve complex problems more effectively, and create a future that is richer, more efficient, and more fulfilling for everyone. It's not about us versus the machines; it's about us *with* the machines, forging a powerful partnership for the benefit of humanity.

Human-AI Symbiosis

Okay, let's really lean into a concept that takes that idea of human-AI collaboration a step further – the exciting and sometimes mind-bending potential of human-AI symbiosis. Now, when you hear "symbiosis," you might think of those cool relationships in nature, like a bee pollinating a flower where both benefit. Human-AI symbiosis is the idea of a much closer, more integrated relationship between us and artificial intelligence, where we essentially become partners in a more profound way, potentially leading to enhancements in both our cognitive and physical abilities. Think of it less like just using a tool and more like merging with a very powerful and intelligent partner.

One of the most immediate and perhaps already subtly emerging forms of this symbiosis is in how we interact with our personal devices and digital assistants. Think about how reliant many of us are on our smartphones for information, navigation, communication, and even managing our daily schedules. AI powers many of these functionalities, learning our preferences and anticipating our needs. This is a very early stage of symbiosis, where AI is already extending our cognitive reach, helping us remember things, find information instantly, and connect with others more easily.

As AI becomes more sophisticated and more deeply integrated into our lives, this symbiotic relationship could become much more profound. Imagine AI companions that truly understand our personalities, our goals, and even our emotional states. They could act as highly personalized advisors, mentors, or even creative collaborators, providing insights, suggesting new perspectives, and helping us to achieve our full potential in various aspects of our lives, from our careers to our personal growth.

Consider the possibilities in education. Imagine AI tutors that are not just personalized but deeply attuned to our individual learning styles and even our emotional responses to different subjects. They could adapt their teaching methods in real-time, provide encouragement when we're struggling, and challenge us in ways that perfectly suit our abilities, leading to a much more effective and engaging learning experience. It's like having a super-patient and incredibly knowledgeable personal tutor available 24/7.

In the realm of creativity, the symbiosis between human artists and AI could lead to entirely new forms of artistic expression. Imagine artists using AI tools that can understand their creative intent and generate novel ideas, suggest unexpected combinations of elements, or even help them to realize complex visions that would be impossible to achieve on their own. It's like having a powerful muse and a tireless assistant all rolled into one.

The potential for human-AI symbiosis extends beyond just our cognitive abilities. Imagine integrating AI more directly with our physical bodies through advanced prosthetics or wearable technology. AI-powered prosthetics could learn and adapt to a user's movements and intentions with incredible precision, potentially restoring or even enhancing physical capabilities. Wearable AI could monitor our health in real-time, providing early warnings of potential problems or even delivering personalized interventions.

Looking further into the future, some speculate about even more direct forms of human-AI integration, perhaps through brain-computer interfaces. While this is still largely in the realm of research and speculation, imagine a future where our thoughts and intentions could directly interact with AI systems, allowing for seamless communication and control of technology with the power of our minds. This could have profound implications for people with disabilities, potentially restoring lost senses or motor functions. It could also potentially lead to a significant augmentation of human cognitive abilities, allowing us to access and process information in entirely new ways.

However, as with any powerful technology, the potential for human-AI symbiosis also comes with significant ethical considerations. We need to think carefully about issues like autonomy – ensuring that we remain in control of our own thoughts and decisions even as we become more closely integrated with AI. Privacy and data security will become even more critical as AI systems gain deeper access to our personal information and even our biological data. Equity and access are also important – we need to ensure that the benefits of human-AI symbiosis are available to everyone and don't exacerbate existing inequalities.

We'll need to grapple with questions about identity and what it means to be human in a world where the lines between biology and technology become increasingly blurred. As we become more intertwined with AI, how will this affect our sense of self and our relationships with each other? These are profound questions that will require careful consideration as this technology evolves.

The potential of human-AI symbiosis is vast and largely uncharted. It offers the tantalizing prospect of augmenting our abilities in ways that could lead to unprecedented progress and understanding. However, realizing this potential in a way that is beneficial and ethical will require careful thought, ongoing dialogue, and a commitment to ensuring that this powerful partnership serves humanity's best interests. It's about forging a future where humans and AI don't just coexist, but thrive together in a truly symbiotic relationship.

Future with Intelligent Systems

So, let's really paint a picture of a future where we're not just using AI as a tool, but actively co-creating our world alongside these intelligent systems. It's a subtle but powerful shift in perspective, moving away from a one-way relationship where we command and AI obeys, towards a more dynamic and collaborative partnership where both humans and AI contribute uniquely to shaping what comes next. Think of it like a jazz ensemble, where different instruments improvise and build upon each other's contributions to create something richer and more innovative than any single player could achieve alone.

One of the most fundamental ways we can co-create with intelligent systems is in the realm of problem-solving. We humans are often good at identifying complex problems, framing them in a broader context, and bringing creativity and intuition to the table. AI, on the other hand, excels at analyzing vast amounts of data, identifying hidden patterns, and exploring a wide range of potential solutions with incredible speed and efficiency. By working together, we can leverage these complementary strengths to tackle challenges that might otherwise seem insurmountable, from finding cures for diseases to developing sustainable solutions for our planet. Imagine a team of human scientists working with an AI that can sift through millions of research papers and experimental results, pinpointing promising avenues of inquiry that a human might miss, while the scientists use their expertise and intuition to design new experiments and interpret the AI's findings.

This co-creation extends beautifully into the realm of innovation. Think about how AI can act as a powerful catalyst for human creativity. We've already touched on AI generating design options or musical ideas. In a co-creative future, this could become much more integrated. An artist might work with an AI that can understand their aesthetic preferences and suggest novel combinations of colors, shapes, or sounds, pushing the boundaries of artistic expression in ways we can't even imagine today. A writer might collaborate with an AI that can help them explore different narrative structures, suggest alternative word choices, or even generate initial drafts of certain sections, freeing the writer to focus on the core themes and emotional depth of their story. It's like having a tireless and incredibly imaginative brainstorming partner who can constantly offer new perspectives and possibilities.

The process of design and engineering could also be fundamentally transformed through co-creation with AI. Imagine architects working with AI that can analyze vast amounts of data on material properties, environmental impact, and structural integrity to generate optimal building designs that are both aesthetically pleasing and highly efficient. Engineers could collaborate with AI that can simulate complex systems and identify potential flaws or areas for improvement far more quickly than traditional methods allow. This kind of partnership could lead to the creation of more sustainable, more efficient, and more human-centered products and infrastructure.

Even in the way we learn and grow, co-creation with intelligent systems holds immense potential. Imagine personalized learning experiences that go far beyond simply adapting the pace of instruction. An AI tutor could understand not just our learning style but also our motivations, our emotional responses to different subjects, and our long-term goals, tailoring the learning journey in a truly holistic way. We could engage in dynamic dialogues with AI systems that can challenge our assumptions, provide us with diverse perspectives, and help us develop critical thinking skills. It's like having a wise and endlessly patient mentor who is always available to guide us on our individual paths of learning and self-discovery.

The concept of co-creation also implies a more reciprocal relationship with AI. As we interact with these intelligent systems, we provide them with feedback, we refine their understanding of the world and our values, and we help them to evolve and become more aligned with our needs and desires. In turn, they provide us with insights, automate tasks that free up our time and energy, and augment our cognitive and physical abilities. It's a continuous feedback loop where both humans and AI are learning and adapting in response to the collaboration.

However, this vision of co-creating the future with intelligent systems also requires us to be mindful of the ethical considerations. We need to ensure that these partnerships are built on principles of transparency, fairness, and accountability. We need to design AI systems that respect human autonomy and agency, rather than simply directing or manipulating us. The goal should be to empower humans through this collaboration, to enhance our capabilities and help us achieve our goals in a more effective and fulfilling way.

The future we co-create with intelligent systems has the potential to be one where human ingenuity and artificial intelligence work in synergy to address some of the world's most pressing challenges, to unlock new frontiers of creativity and innovation, and to enhance the human experience in profound ways. It's about moving beyond the idea of AI as a mere tool and embracing the possibility of a true partnership, where our combined intelligence can shape a future that is more prosperous, more sustainable, and more meaningful for all. It's like embarking on an exciting journey together, with both humans and AI contributing their unique talents to navigate the path ahead and build the world we want to live in.

Chapter 9: The AI Journey

Now, let's take a step back for a moment and just reflect on this whole "AI journey" we've been on, even if you're just starting to get a sense of what it's all about. It's been a pretty remarkable ride so far, and when you look at where we started, where we are now, and where we might be heading, it's quite something to think about.

If you rewind the clock a few decades, the idea of truly intelligent machines was largely confined to the realm of science fiction. We had computers that could perform calculations and automate tasks, but the notion of a machine that could learn, reason, and understand the world in a human-like way seemed like a distant dream. The early days of AI research were filled with both excitement and significant challenges. There were initial bursts of optimism, followed by periods known as "AI winters" when progress seemed to stall and funding dried up. It was a time of exploring different approaches, many of which ultimately hit dead ends.

But then, something started to shift. The confluence of several key factors – the availability of vast amounts of data, the increasing power of computing hardware, and breakthroughs in new algorithms, particularly in the field of deep learning – sparked a resurgence in AI research and development. Suddenly, those long-held dreams started to feel a little bit closer. We saw AI achieve impressive feats in areas like image recognition, natural language processing, and game playing, things that many experts thought were still decades away.

Looking at where we are now, AI is no longer just a research topic; it's becoming increasingly integrated into our everyday lives. From the recommendation systems that suggest our next movie to watch or song to listen to, to the virtual assistants that answer our questions and manage our schedules, AI is quietly working behind the scenes in countless applications. It's being used in healthcare to help doctors diagnose diseases, in transportation to develop self-driving cars, in manufacturing to automate processes, and in countless other industries to improve efficiency and create new possibilities.

It's been a journey of constant learning and adaptation. Researchers have built upon previous ideas, learned from failures, and continuously pushed the boundaries of what's possible. We've seen the rise of powerful new techniques and the development of sophisticated tools and frameworks that make it easier for developers to build and deploy AI models. The field has become incredibly diverse and interdisciplinary, drawing on expertise from computer science, mathematics, linguistics, neuroscience, and many other areas.

But this journey hasn't been without its bumps in the road. We've grappled with ethical concerns around bias in AI, the implications for privacy and surveillance, and the potential impact on jobs and the economy. These are complex issues that require careful consideration and ongoing dialogue as AI continues to evolve and become more deeply woven into the fabric of our society.

As we look ahead, the future of the AI journey is full of both immense potential and significant uncertainty. We're still striving to achieve Artificial General Intelligence (AGI), that elusive goal of creating AI with human-level cognitive abilities. Whether and when we will reach that milestone is still a matter of debate, but the pursuit of AGI continues to drive much of the cutting-edge research in the field.

Beyond AGI, there's the exciting and sometimes daunting prospect of superintelligence – AI that surpasses human intelligence across all domains. While this is still largely in the realm of speculation, the potential implications are so profound that it warrants serious consideration. Ensuring that any future superintelligence remains aligned with human values and goals is one of the most critical challenges facing the field.

The journey of AI is also increasingly becoming one of collaboration – not just between researchers and developers, but between humans and AI systems themselves. As AI becomes more sophisticated, the potential for a true symbiosis, where we work together in a more integrated way, could unlock entirely new levels of human potential and innovation.

Reflecting on this journey, it's clear that AI is not just a technological advancement; it's a force that is reshaping our world in profound ways. It's a journey of continuous discovery, with new possibilities and challenges emerging all the time. And while the path ahead may not always be clear, the potential rewards of harnessing the power of intelligent systems for the benefit of humanity are immense. It's a journey we're all on together, and it's one that will undoubtedly continue to surprise and challenge us in the years to come.

Changing the World

Let's settle in and really think about something that's happening all around us, often so subtly we barely notice it: how Artificial Intelligence is quietly but profoundly reshaping the very way we live our lives and even the way we think. It's not just about robots taking over jobs in some distant future; it's happening right here, right now, in ways both big and small.

Think about how you start your day. Maybe you ask a smart speaker about the weather or the news. That's AI at work, understanding your voice and retrieving information for you. When you check your social media feeds, the content you see is often curated by AI algorithms designed to show you things you might find interesting. When you search for something online, AI powers the search engine, understanding your query and sifting through billions of web pages to find the most relevant results. These are just the tip of the iceberg.

AI is increasingly influencing how we communicate. Think about translation apps that allow people speaking different languages to understand each other in real-time. Or consider the predictive text on your phone, which learns your writing style and suggests words as you type, subtly shaping how you formulate your sentences. Even the way we interact with customer service is changing, with AI-powered chatbots handling many initial inquiries, learning from each interaction to provide more efficient support.

Our work lives are also being transformed. In many industries, AI is automating repetitive tasks, freeing up human workers to focus on more creative and strategic work. Think about AI in manufacturing, controlling robots on assembly lines with incredible precision. Or AI in finance, analyzing vast amounts of data to identify trends and manage risk. Even in fields like law and journalism, AI is being used to assist with tasks like document review and news aggregation, augmenting human capabilities and changing the nature of these professions.

The way we learn and access information is also undergoing a revolution. AI-powered educational tools can personalize learning experiences, adapting to individual student needs and providing tailored feedback. Online learning platforms use AI to recommend courses and resources based on your interests and learning history. The sheer volume of information available to us is being navigated and filtered by AI systems, shaping what we see and ultimately what we learn.

Even our leisure time is increasingly influenced by AI. Streaming services use AI to recommend movies and TV shows based on our viewing history. Music platforms suggest new artists and songs we might enjoy. Video games are becoming more immersive and responsive thanks to AI-powered non-player characters and dynamically generated content. It's like having an AI concierge constantly tailoring our entertainment experiences.

Perhaps more subtly, AI is even starting to influence how we think. The constant stream of information filtered and presented to us by AI algorithms can shape our perspectives and even our understanding of the world. If we primarily see news and opinions that align with our existing beliefs, as often happens with social media algorithms, it can create filter bubbles and reinforce our biases. This isn't necessarily a conscious choice we're making, but rather a consequence of how these AI systems are designed to keep us engaged.

The increasing reliance on AI for decision-making, even in seemingly small ways, can also subtly shift our own cognitive habits. If we constantly rely on AI to remind us of things or to provide us with quick answers, we might become less reliant on our own memory and problem-solving skills. It's like constantly using a calculator – while it's convenient, it might also lead to a decline in our mental arithmetic abilities if we don't actively engage those skills.

The very nature of trust and authority is being challenged and redefined in the age of AI. When an AI system provides information or makes a recommendation, how do we determine its reliability? How do we understand its biases? As we interact more with AI that can generate increasingly realistic text, images, and even videos, the ability to discern what is real and what is artificially created becomes a critical skill. This requires us to develop new forms of critical thinking and media literacy in an AI-driven world.

The ongoing development of AI also raises profound philosophical questions about the nature of intelligence, consciousness, and what it means to be human. As AI systems become more sophisticated, we are forced to confront our own assumptions about what makes us unique. This introspection, sparked by the progress in AI, can itself reshape our understanding of ourselves and our place in the universe.

The reshaping of how we live and think by AI is an ongoing and evolving process. It's not a sudden, dramatic shift, but rather a gradual integration of intelligent systems into the fabric of our daily lives. It offers incredible opportunities for convenience, efficiency, and new forms of knowledge and creativity. However, it also presents challenges that we need to address thoughtfully and proactively, ensuring that we remain mindful of the ethical implications and actively shape the future of AI in a way that benefits humanity as a whole. It's about understanding this powerful force and learning to live and think alongside it in a way that enhances our lives and our understanding of the world around us.

Inspiring the Next Generation of AI Innovators

Alright, let's talk about something really close to my heart: how we can get the next generation excited about and involved in the incredible world of Artificial Intelligence. It's not just about training future coders; it's about sparking curiosity, fostering creativity, and empowering young minds to become the AI innovators of tomorrow. Think of it like planting seeds in fertile ground – we need to cultivate their interest and provide them with the right tools and encouragement to grow into the brilliant minds that will shape the future of AI.

One of the most crucial things we can do is to demystify AI. For many young people, AI might seem like something abstract, complicated, or even a little scary, fueled by science fiction portrayals. We need to show them that at its core, AI is about problem-solving using computers in clever ways. We can start by introducing them to everyday examples of AI that they already interact with – things like the voice assistant on their phone, the recommendations on their favorite streaming service, or even the filters on social media. By showing them that AI is already a part of their lives in helpful and often fun ways, we can make it feel more accessible and less like some futuristic, unattainable concept.

We also need to emphasize the creative potential of AI. It's not just about algorithms and code; it's about using these tools to build new things, solve real-world problems, and even express artistic ideas. We can encourage young people to think about challenges they see around them – in their schools, their communities, or even globally – and how AI might offer solutions. This could involve brainstorming ideas for AI-powered apps that help the environment, tools that make learning more engaging, or systems that improve accessibility for people with disabilities. The key is to frame AI not just as a subject to be studied, but as a powerful tool for innovation and positive change.

Making learning about AI engaging and hands-on is absolutely vital. Instead of just dry lectures and abstract theories, we need to provide opportunities for young people to actually build and experiment with AI concepts. This could involve using visual programming languages that make it easy to create simple AI applications, working with robotics kits that incorporate AI for tasks like object recognition or navigation, or even participating in coding challenges and competitions focused on AI. There are increasingly accessible tools and platforms available that allow even beginners to get their hands dirty and see AI in action. It's like learning to bake – reading recipes is helpful, but actually mixing the ingredients and seeing the cake rise is what truly sparks your interest.

We should also highlight the interdisciplinary nature of AI. It's not just for computer science whizzes. AI draws on ideas from mathematics, statistics, psychology, linguistics, ethics, and many other fields. This means that students with a wide range of interests and skills can find a place in the world of AI. We can encourage young people to explore the connections between AI and their other passions, whether it's art, music, biology, or social justice. For example, someone interested in environmental science could explore how AI is being used for climate modeling or conservation efforts. Someone passionate about language could delve into natural language processing. Showing these connections can broaden the appeal of AI and attract a more diverse group of future innovators.

It's also crucial to foster a sense of community and collaboration among young people interested in AI. Creating opportunities for them to connect with each other, share ideas, and work on projects together can be incredibly motivating and can help them learn from one another. This could involve setting up AI clubs in schools, organizing workshops and hackathons for young learners, and connecting them with mentors who are already working in the field. Learning alongside peers who share your interests can make the journey much more engaging and supportive.

We need to showcase diverse role models in the field of AI. When young people see individuals from various backgrounds succeeding in AI, it helps them envision themselves in those roles. Highlighting the contributions of women, people of color, and individuals with different life experiences can make the field feel more inclusive and welcoming to everyone. It's important to challenge stereotypes and show that AI innovation comes from a wide range of perspectives.

We need to emphasize the ethical considerations of AI from the very beginning. As we empower the next generation to build intelligent systems, we also need to equip them with a strong ethical compass. This involves teaching them about issues like bias, fairness, privacy, and the responsible use of AI. Encouraging them to think critically about the potential societal impacts of their creations is essential for ensuring that the AI of the future is developed and used in a way that benefits humanity as a whole.

Inspiring the next generation of AI innovators is about nurturing curiosity, fostering creativity, providing hands-on learning experiences, highlighting interdisciplinary connections, building communities, showcasing diverse role models, and instilling a strong ethical foundation. By creating an environment where young people feel empowered, supported, and inspired, we can pave the way for a future where AI is developed and used by a diverse and passionate group of individuals who are committed to creating a better world. It's an investment in the future, and the potential returns are immense.

Curiosity, Responsibility, and Innovation

Okay, let's have a really important heart-to-heart about three things that are absolutely vital, not just in the world of AI, but in pretty much every aspect of life: encouraging curiosity, fostering responsibility, and igniting innovation. Think of these as the three legs of a sturdy stool – if any one of them is weak, the whole thing becomes unstable. And as we navigate this increasingly AI-driven world, nurturing these qualities in ourselves and especially in the next generation is more crucial than ever.

First, let's talk about curiosity. At its heart, curiosity is that innate desire to learn, to explore, to ask "why?" and "what if?". It's the spark that ignites the flame of discovery. In the context of AI, and really any complex field, curiosity is what drives us to understand how things work, to delve deeper into the underlying principles, and to not just accept things at face value. For someone new to AI, fostering curiosity might start with simply asking "How does that voice assistant on my phone actually understand what I'm saying?" or "What are the limits of what these AI systems can do?". Encouraging this kind of questioning is the first step towards genuine understanding and engagement.

How do we nurture curiosity? I think it starts with creating an environment where questions are welcomed, not dismissed. It means encouraging exploration without the fear of failure. Sometimes, the most valuable learning comes from trying things that don't quite work out. It's about providing resources and opportunities for people to explore their interests, whether it's through hands-on projects, engaging content, or simply having open and encouraging conversations. Think about a child taking apart a toy to see how it works – that's curiosity in action. We need to maintain that spirit of inquiry as we grow and as we encounter new and complex topics like AI.

Next up is responsibility. As we become more capable, as we gain more knowledge and power (and AI is certainly a powerful tool), the importance of responsibility grows exponentially. In the context of AI, responsibility encompasses a wide range of considerations. It means thinking critically about the ethical implications of the AI systems we create and use. It involves being mindful of potential biases in algorithms and working to mitigate them. It requires us to consider the impact of AI on society, on jobs, on privacy, and on the environment. It's about asking not just "can we do this?" but "should we do this?" and "what are the potential consequences?".

Fostering responsibility, especially in those who are learning about and building AI, is paramount. This involves education about ethical frameworks, about the potential for misuse of technology, and about the importance of considering the broader societal impact of their work. It means encouraging a mindset of accountability and transparency. Just like a skilled driver needs to understand the rules of the road and the potential dangers of irresponsible driving, those who work with AI need to understand the ethical guidelines and the potential for harm if these powerful tools are not used wisely.

We have innovation. Innovation is about taking that curiosity and that sense of responsibility and channeling them into creating new and better solutions. It's about thinking outside the box, challenging existing paradigms, and finding novel ways to address problems and create value. In the field of AI, innovation is what drives the development of new algorithms, new applications, and new ways for humans and machines to interact. It's about looking at the world with a sense of "what could be?" and then using our knowledge and skills to bring those possibilities to life.

How do we ignite innovation? I believe it stems from the fertile ground of curiosity and is guided by a strong sense of responsibility. When people are naturally curious and feel a sense of ownership over the impact of their work, they are more likely to think creatively and come up with novel solutions. Providing opportunities for experimentation, for collaboration, and for taking calculated risks can foster a culture of innovation. It's about creating a space where new ideas are not only welcomed but actively encouraged, and where the focus is on continuous improvement and pushing the boundaries of what's possible. Think about the great inventors throughout history – their curiosity about how things worked, coupled with a desire to solve problems, led to groundbreaking innovations.

These three qualities – curiosity, responsibility, and innovation – are deeply interconnected. Curiosity fuels the desire to learn and explore, which in turn can lead to innovative ideas. Responsibility guides that innovation, ensuring that it is directed towards positive and ethical outcomes. And the process of innovation itself often sparks further curiosity and a deeper sense of responsibility for the impact of our creations.

As we move further into an age increasingly shaped by AI, nurturing these qualities in everyone, especially those who will be the architects of this future, is absolutely essential. It's not just about creating more powerful AI; it's about creating a future where that power is wielded with wisdom, guided by a deep sense of responsibility, and driven by a relentless curiosity to make the world a better place. It's a shared endeavor, and by encouraging these fundamental human qualities, we can ensure that the AI journey is one that leads to progress and prosperity for all.

Chapter 10: FAQs About AI for Beginners

Let's tackle some of those burning questions you might have about Artificial Intelligence, especially if it feels like a whole new world. Don't worry, it's not as intimidating as it might sound, and hopefully, by the time we're done here, you'll have a much clearer picture of what AI is all about. Think of this as a friendly chat where we clear up some of the most common curiosities.

So, the big one right off the bat is usually: What exactly *is* Artificial Intelligence? In simple terms, it's about getting computers to do things that normally require human intelligence. This can include things like learning, problem-solving, decision-making, understanding language, and recognizing patterns. It's not about creating robots that look and act exactly like humans (though that's a part of science fiction!), but rather about building systems that can perform tasks that we typically associate with our own intelligence.

Now, you might be wondering: Is AI just one thing, or are there different kinds? That's a great question! The AI we see in movies, often called "general AI" or AGI, which has human-level intelligence across the board, doesn't really exist yet. What we have today is mostly "narrow AI" or "weak AI." This kind of AI is designed to be really good at specific tasks. Think of the AI that recommends movies on a streaming service – it's very good at figuring out what you might like to watch based on your past behavior, but it can't suddenly start driving a car or writing a poem. So, for now, AI is usually specialized.

Another common question is: How does AI actually *learn*? This often involves something called "machine learning." Imagine teaching a dog a new trick. You show it what to do, and if it gets it right, you give it a treat. Over time, the dog learns to associate the action with the reward. Machine learning works in a similar way, but with data. We feed computers large amounts of data, and they learn to identify patterns and make predictions or decisions based on that data. There are different ways this learning happens, but the basic idea is that the AI gets better at its task over time as it processes more and more information.

You might also hear the term "deep learning" a lot. How is that different from regular machine learning? Deep learning is a type of machine learning that uses artificial neural networks with many layers (hence "deep"). These networks are inspired by the structure of the human brain and are particularly good at learning complex patterns from large amounts of unstructured data, like images, audio, and text. Think of it as a more sophisticated and powerful way for AI to learn, allowing it to tackle more complex problems like understanding natural language or recognizing objects in images with very high accuracy.

A lot of people also ask: Is AI going to take all our jobs? This is a big concern for many, and it's understandable. AI definitely has the potential to automate many tasks that are currently done by humans, especially those that are repetitive or routine. However, many experts believe that while some jobs will be displaced, AI will also create new jobs that don't exist today, particularly in fields related to developing, implementing, and maintaining AI systems. It's likely that the nature of work will change, requiring people to adapt and learn new skills to work alongside AI. It's more about a shift in the job market than a complete disappearance of work, though we'll need to think carefully about how to manage this transition.

Then there's the question of AI ethics. Are there rules for how AI should be developed and used? Absolutely, and this is a really important and growing area of discussion. As AI becomes more powerful and more integrated into our lives, we need to think carefully about the ethical implications. This includes things like ensuring AI systems are fair and don't perpetuate biases, protecting people's privacy when AI uses their data, and making sure there's accountability when AI systems make mistakes. There's a lot of work being done to establish ethical guidelines and even regulations for AI development and deployment.

You might also be curious about how AI is used in everyday life right now. We've touched on a few examples, but it's really all around us. Think about the spam filter in your email, the GPS navigation in your car, the fraud detection systems that protect your bank accounts, and the personalized recommendations you get on e-commerce websites. AI is already making our lives more convenient, efficient, and sometimes even safer in countless ways, often without us even realizing it.

Another question that often comes up is: How is AI different from just regular software? Regular software follows a set of pre-programmed rules. It does exactly what it's been told to do. AI, on the other hand, has the ability to learn and adapt based on the data it processes. It can improve its performance over time without being explicitly reprogrammed for every single scenario. This ability to learn and evolve is a key characteristic that sets AI apart.

Many people wonder: What does the future of AI look like? That's a really exciting but also somewhat uncertain question. We're likely to see AI become even more integrated into our lives, becoming more sophisticated and capable. We might see advancements towards more general AI, though exactly when and how that might happen is still up for debate. The potential for AI to solve complex problems, drive innovation, and transform industries is enormous. However, it's crucial that we continue to develop and deploy AI responsibly, with careful consideration of its ethical and societal implications, to ensure that it benefits all of humanity.

So, there you have it – a little peek into some of the most common questions people have about AI. It's a fascinating and rapidly evolving field, and while it can seem complex at first, the basic ideas are often quite intuitive. The key is to keep asking questions and to stay curious as AI continues to shape the world around us.

www.ingramcontent.com/pod-product-compliance
Lightning Source LLC
LaVergne TN
LVHW051443050326
832903LV00030BD/3224